Promoting Enterprise Digitalisation in Azerbaijan

))OECD

BETTER POLICIES FOR BETTER LIVES

This work is published under the responsibility of the Secretary-General of the OECD. The opinions expressed and arguments employed herein do not necessarily reflect the official views of the Member countries of the OECD.

This document, as well as any data and map included herein, are without prejudice to the status of or sovereignty over any territory, to the delimitation of international frontiers and boundaries and to the name of any territory, city or area.

Please cite this publication as:
OECD (2022), *Promoting Enterprise Digitalisation in Azerbaijan* , OECD Publishing, Paris, https://doi.org/10.1787/6a612a2a-en.

ISBN 978-92-64-42229-2 (print)
ISBN 978-92-64-87094-9 (pdf)
ISBN 978-92-64-86229-6 (HTML)
ISBN 978-92-64-33788-6 (epub)

Foreword

The Government of Azerbaijan has been prioritising economic diversification, private sector development and entrepreneurship over the past years and made significant progress in establishing an institutional framework for SME development. The COVID-19 crisis has given renewed urgency to further strengthen these efforts, in particular to support the digitalisation of SMEs. However, many SMEs lag behind larger firms in the digital transition as a result of important barriers with respect to skills, innovation, infrastructure, regulation and finance, among other things. They are often unaware of the opportunities to increase productivity and competitiveness, cannot clearly identify their digitalisation needs, and lack the financial means to embed digital tools in their operations. The SME digital gap slows productivity growth and increases inequalities among people, firms and places. In addition, SMEs often fail to exploit the opportunities offered by e-commerce and their digital marketing activities lack professionalism and strategic planning.

In this context, the Government of Azerbaijan requested the OECD's assistance in supporting the design and implementation of strategies and policies to foster the digital transformation of Azerbaijan's SME sector. The main objective of this project is to promote SME digitalisation by providing tailored guidance to policy makers through a combination of research, analysis, benchmarking of good practices with OECD member countries and targeted capacity building activities.

The main direct beneficiaries of this project are the Ministry of Economy, the Small and Medium Business Development Agency, and other ministries, agencies and key stakeholders involved in the design, implementation and monitoring of SME policies in Azerbaijan. The ultimate beneficiaries are Azerbaijan's SMEs and entrepreneurs, as well as their employees and customers.

This note, which summarises project findings, served as a basis for discussion during a peer review of Azerbaijan at the OECD Eurasia Competitiveness Roundtable on 23 November 2021 and is structured as follows: Chapter 1 provides an overview of the role of SMEs in Azerbaijan's economy and the latest SME policy developments. Chapter 2 looks closely at the strategic approach to SME digitalisation policy and the institutional framework for SME development. Chapter 3 assesses the digital infrastructure and regulatory environment as well as digital skills among the population. Chapter 4 offers an analysis of financial and non-financial services to support the adoption of digital technologies by SMEs, and finally, Chapter 5 provides policy considerations to address some of the identified policy barriers.

The work has been carried out with the support of regular meetings of a public-private Working Group to determine policy priorities and identify gaps in reform implementation. In addition, the OECD has carried out an extensive series of bilateral interviews with representatives of the public and private sector.

The project is carried out as part of the multi-country project *EU4Business: From Policies to Action – Phase 2*, implemented by the OECD in the Eastern Partnership, with the financial support of the European Union under its EU4Business initiative.

Acknowledgements

This report summarises the work carried out by the OECD Eurasia Competitiveness Programme (ECP) under the authority of the OECD Eastern Europe and South Caucasus Initiative Steering Committee, in consultation with the government of the Republic of Azerbaijan and with participation of private sector and international organisations in Azerbaijan.

Representatives from several ministries, government agencies, private sector organisations, and other stakeholders should be acknowledged for their active participation in working group meetings and their availability to meet with the OECD team and share valuable insights for the development of this note.

In particular, the OECD would like to extend its gratitude to the representatives of the Ministry of Economy of the Republic of Azerbaijan: Mr Mikayil Jabbarov (Minister of Economy), Mr Rovshan Najaf (Deputy Minister of Economy), Ms Inara Mustafayeva (Head of Department for International Co-operation) and Ms Farida Mammadova (Department for International Co-operation). The OECD is also very grateful to representatives of the Small and Medium Business Development Agency (SMBDA): Mr Mehman Abbas (Former Deputy Chairman), Mr Elmar Isayev (Head of Secretariat) and Mr Amir Shirinbayli (Head of International Cooperation Department).

The OECD is also very grateful to representatives of the project advisory group, who provided useful inputs to the working group discussions that contributed to this report: Mr Tamerlan Taghiyev (Director of the Centre for Analysis and Coordination of the 4IR, Ministry of Economy of Azerbaijan), Ms Leyla Mammadova (Deputy Chair of the Agency for Agro Credit and Development, Ministry of Agriculture of Azerbaijan), Mr Eldar Jahangirov (Team Leader, Ministry of Digital Development and Transport of Azerbaijan), Mr Farid Osmanov (Executive Director, Central Bank of Azerbaijan), Mr Mehdi Javadov (Deputy Director, ASAN), Mr Nuru Suleymanov (Director of the Department of National Accounts and Macroeconomic Statistics, Azerbaijan State Statistical Committee), and Mr Vugar Zeynalov (Vice President of the National Confederation of Entrepreneurs Organisations of Azerbaijan).

The European Union co-financed this project as part of the EU4Business initiative and its staff provided important guidance and support: Mr Mathieu Bousquet (Deputy Director, DG NEAR), Ms Diana Jablonska (Head of Unit, DG NEAR), Mr Lucian Jega (Programme Assistant, DG NEAR) and the representatives of the EU Delegation to the Republic of Azerbaijan: Mr Peter Michalko (Ambassador) Mr Kestutis Jankauskas (former Ambassador), Ms Simona Gatti (former Head of Operations Section), and Ms Ulvyia Abdullayeva (Programme Manager).

This report was written under the guidance of Mr Andreas Schaal (Director, OECD Global Relations) and Mr William Tompson (Head, OECD Eurasia Division).

The principal authors of this report are Mr Patrik Pruzinsky and Ms Maria Zelenova (Policy Analysts, OECD Global Relations Secretariat). The project was managed by Mr Daniel Quadbeck and this report was reviewed by Mr Jorge Gálvez Mendéz (OECD Global Relations Secretariat).

Very valuable administrative support was provided by Ms Mariana Tanova (OECD Global Relations Secretariat).

Table of contents

Acronyms and abbreviations

ABAD	ASAN Support to Family Business
AKIA	Agency for Agro Credit and Development
ASAN	Azerbaijani Service and Assessment
ASXM	ASAN Certification Services Centre
AZN	Azerbaijani Manat
BMDW	Austrian Federal Ministry of Digitalisation and Business Location
B2B	Business to Business
B2C	Business to Consumer
B2G	Business to Government
CC	Cloud Computing
CDISE	Austrian Data & IT Security Expert
CERT	Computer Incident Response Team
CIS	Commonwealth of Independent States
CRM	Customer Relations Management
DTS	Digital Transformation Strategy
EaP	Eastern Partnership
ESC	Electronic and Security Centre
ESG	Enterprise Singapore
ERP	Enterprise Resource Planning
EU	European Union
EU-8	Czech Republic, Estonia, Hungary, Latvia, Lithuania, Poland, Slovakia, Slovenia
EUR	Euro
FDI	Foreign Direct Investment
GDP	Gross Domestic Product
G2B	Government to Business
ICT	Information and Communication Technology
IDP	Industry Digital Plans

IMDA	Singapore's Infocomm Media Development Authority
ITU	International Telecommunication Union
IVET`	Initial Vocational Education and Training
KMU	Austrian Institute for SME Research
KPI	Key Performance Indicators
MDL	Moldovan Leu
MDDT	Ministry of Digital Development and Transport
NQF	National Quality Framework
NRA	National Regulatory Body
ODIMM	Moldovan Organisation for Small and Medium-Sized Enterprises Sector Development
OECD	Organisation for Economic Co-operation and Development
PISA	OECD's Programme for International Student Assessment
PKI	Public Key Infrastructure
PSG	Productivity Solutions Grant
RFID	Radio Frequency Identification
SAPSSI	State Agency for Public Services and Social Innovations
SMBDA	Small and Medium Business Development Agency of Azerbaijan
SCM	Supply-Chain Management
SME	Small and Medium Enterprises
STEM	Science, Technology, Engineering and Math
UN	United Nations
USAID	United States Agency for International Development
USD	US Dollars
VET	Vocational Education and Training
WKO	Austrian Chamber of Commerce

Executive summary

Azerbaijan's economy was significantly affected by the COVID-19 pandemic. In 2020, Azerbaijan's gross domestic product (GDP) contracted by 4.3% due to the economic shock of the pandemic and related business closures. The crisis has had a particularly negative impact on small and medium-sized enterprises (SMEs), which remain an untapped source of economic development in Azerbaijan with only 14.9% share of value added and 45% share of employment in 2019. This is a significantly lower contribution compared to OECD and other Eastern Partnership (EaP) countries.

Since 2015, Azerbaijan made significant progress in improving the business environment for SMEs, by reforming the operational and regulatory environment and strengthening the institutional support for SME development through the establishment of the Small and Medium Business Development Agency and the Innovation and Digital Development Agency. However, a significant gap remains with regards to the digital transformation of SMEs. A discernible digital divide still exists within Azerbaijan, with relatively low levels of broadband connectivity and significant regional differences. Moreover, digital skills gap among the population and, in certain areas, the slow pace of regulatory environment reforms prevent more rapid adoption of digital solutions by SMEs and the general population. SMEs in Azerbaijan are also lagging behind regional peers and OECD members in adopting digital solutions and the range of support services offered for SMEs aimed at promoting digitalisation in non-information and communication technolgy (ICT) sectors remains limited.

While several strategic policy documents envisage implementation of policies supporting digitalisation, a national digitalisation strategy has not yet been adopted, which prevents a more comprehensive and co-ordinated approach to SME digitalisation. Digitalisation has the potential to help SMEs tap into new markets, lower operational costs, increase productivity and ultimately boost their profitability and competitiveness. Promoting SME digitalisation calls for measures that will improve policy co-ordination, enable SMEs to access digital infrastructure, improve regulatory environment, boost digital skills and provide SMEs with targeted financial and non-financial programmes boosting adoption of digital solutions.

Table 1. Summary of policy considerations: way forward

Objective	Recommendation	Way forward
Objective 1: Putting digitalisation at the centre of SME policy making	Leverage "Azerbaijan 2030 Vision" to boost SME digitalisation	• Adopt a National Digitalisation Strategy that would set priorities and objectives for digitalisation, including for the SME sector • Include digitalisation-specific policy actions in the mid-term strategies • Establish process- and result-oriented key performance indicators (KPIs) for each policy action
	Improve co-ordination among institutions responsible for digital transformation	• Establish a Digitalisation Commission that would bring together institutions responsible for the digitalisation agenda • Promote policy coherence and co-ordination
	Improve data collection on SME digitalisation	• Expand the range of collected SME digitalisation-related data • Focus on diffusion of digital technologies among SMEs, cybersecurity and e-commerce • Disaggregate data by enterprise size and sector where possible and relevant

Objective	Recommendation	Way forward
Objective 2: Creating framework conditions for SME digitalisation	Improve SME access to digital infrastructure	• Foster accessibility of broadband (quality and affordability) • Reduce unnecessary regulatory barriers and promote competition and policies enabling investment into digital infrastructure • Ensure independence of the recently established National Regulatory Agency and provide it with sufficient financial and human resources
	Strengthen the regulatory framework for digitalisation	• Adopt a National Cybersecurity Strategy • Foster adoption of cybersecurity measures by SMEs by, for example, establishing a national certification scheme for digital security • Foster utilisation of e-government services and promote their inter-operability • Increase financial inclusion and strengthen logistics for e-commerce • Improve customer protection
	Support digitalisation skills development among students and general population	• Conduct skills needs assessments accompanied by skills anticipation exercise • Implement complex education programmes to increase general numeracy and science skills among students • Develop policies to address digital skills requirements mong general population • Increase awareness among SMEs and general population about availability of training and education opportunities
Objective 3: Promoting the adoption of digital solutions by SMEs	Promote digital culture and increase digital awareness among entrepreneurs	• Implement programmes to promote digital awareness • Communicate to entrepreneurs and managers the benefits and risks associated with the adoption of digital solutions
	Understand SME digitalisation needs	• Deepen the scope of the survey implemented by the SMBDA among SMEs on barriers to their growth and operations • Launch an online digital maturity self-assessment tool
	Reinforce provision of non-financial support services	• Increase the provision of training and advisory services to boost adoption of digital solutions by SMEs • Small and Medium Business Development Agency of Azerbaijan (SMBDA) could implement complex digitalisation-specific programmes combining financial and non-financial support
	Boost financial support for SME digitalisation	• Improve ability of SMEs to access external financing • Entrepreneurship Development Fund and SMBDA could consider expanding existing financial support programmes or launch new initiatives targeting SME digitalisation • Improve regulatory framework to support the uptake of alternative sources of external financing
	Ensure high quality of provided support services	• Systematically monitor and evaluate existing support programmes • Ensure that selected external providers meet qualification criteria to deliver their tasks in the required quality • SMBDA could provide SME development centres with methodological guidelines on the delivery of support services
	Leverage existing business and innovation support infrastructure to create eco-system conductive to digitalisation	• Improve co-ordination among innovation agents and involve the private sector in the design and delivery of support programmes (e.g. business associations) • Monitor all existing initiatives and direct SMEs toward relevant programmes

Introduction

Azerbaijan was significantly affected by the COVID-19 pandemic

Azerbaijan reported its first COVID-19 case in early March 2020, shortly after the virus started spreading across Europe. After a slow-down of reported new cases during the summer 2020, the second wave of the pandemic in Azerbaijan reached the peak in December 2020. As of June 2021, Azerbaijan had reported 33,000 cases in total and 490 deaths per million inhabitants. Overall, the officially reported death toll as of August 2021 stood at 5039 COVID-19 deaths. Compared to other EaP countries, Azerbaijan reported the lowest number of COVID-19 cases relative to the size of its population (see Figure 1 Figure 2). Estimates of excess mortality suggest that the actual impact of COVID-19 was substantially greater.[1]

Figure 1. Reported COVID-19 cases in EaP countries

Cumulative number of reported COVID-19 cases per million inhabitants

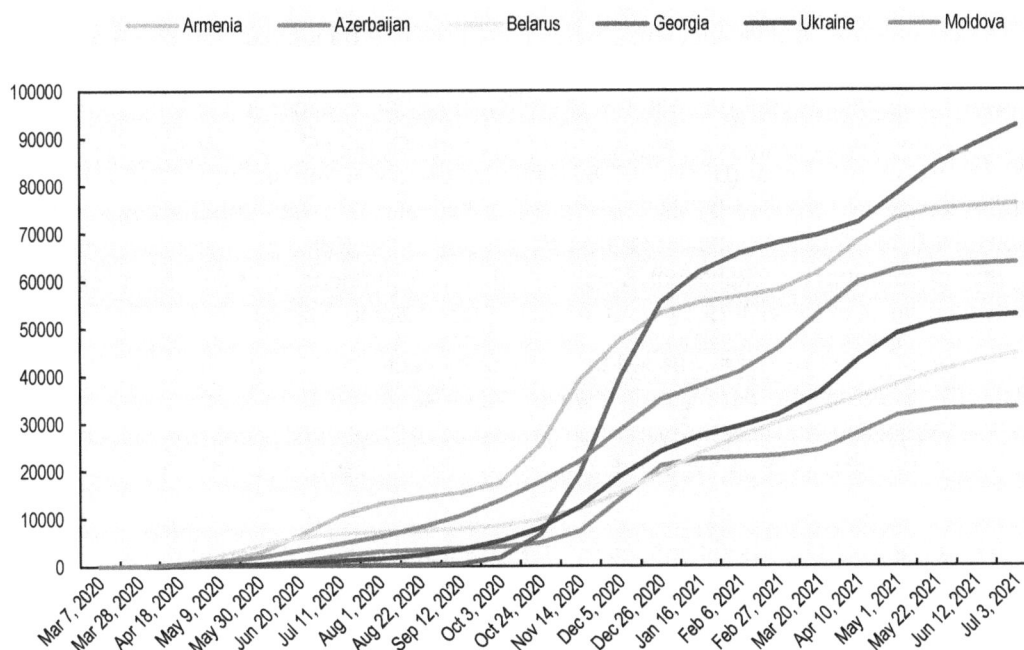

Source: (Worldometer, 2021[1]).

---

[1] In 2020, the total number of deaths from all was about 27.8% above the average for the 2015-19. During January-July 2021, total mortality was around 23.7% above the average for the corresponding periods in 2015-19. This suggests an incidence comparable to that seen in some other Eastern Partner countries, all which show far higher levels of excess mortality than officially reported COVID deaths (Source: World Mortality Dataset, State Statistical Committee of the Republic of Azerbaijan).

Figure 2. Reported COVID-19 deaths in EaP countries

Cumulative number of reported COVID-19 deaths per million inhabitants

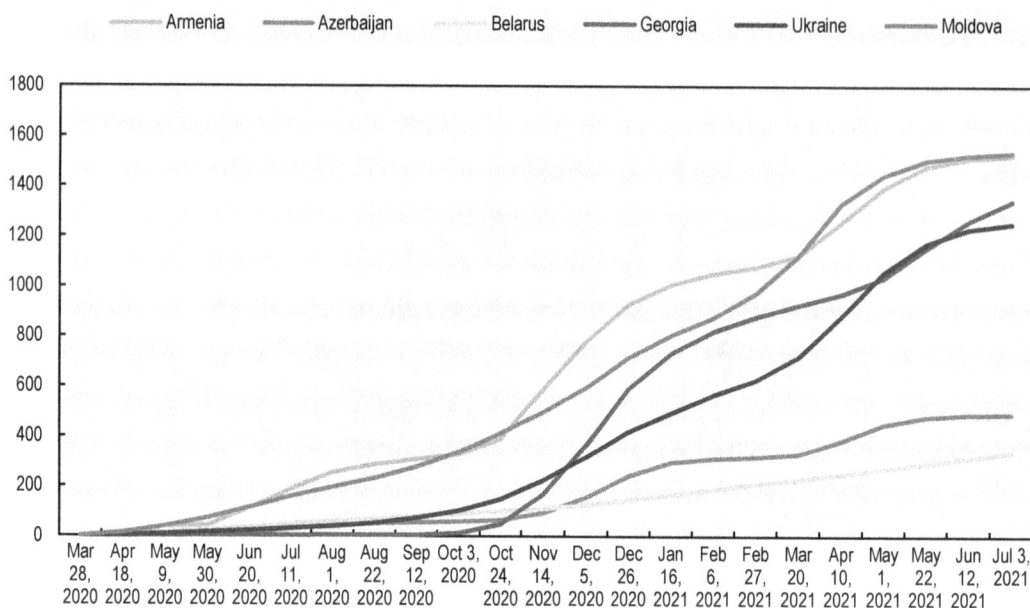

Source: (Worldometer, 2021[1]).

Azerbaijan's economy was significantly affected by the COVID-19 pandemic. In 2020, Azerbaijan's GDP contracted by 4.3% due to the economic shock of the COVID-19 pandemic and related business closures. Border closures disrupted trade flows, and the sharp fall in global oil prices led to the contraction of GDP growth. Strong containment measures also led to a loss of economic activity of around Azerbaijani Manat (AZN) 120-150 million (US Dollar (USD) 70.7-88.4 million) per day in the spring of 2020 (OECD, 2020[2]). Foreign trade turnover decreased by 21.2% in the first half of 2020, with imports down by 42.8% and exports down by 6.1%. Since Azerbaijan is the only country in the EaP that maintains a fixed exchange rate, the loss of revenue put significant pressure on public finances. In total, 5.7% of firms closed permanently as a result of COVID-19 by summer 2021 (World Bank, 2021[3]).

In the first half of 2021, the recovery was led by non-energy sector growth, and it is predicted to continue as more COVID-19 restrictions were lifted. However, some sectors that were particularly hard-hit by the pandemic, such as tourism and hospitality, remain depressed. As higher oil prices are expected to underpin economic growth in 2021, GDP is expected to grow by 5.0% in 2021 and 3.1% in 2022 (World Bank, 2021[4]).

The crisis had a particularly powerful impact on SMEs, which made up the great majority of enterprises that closed permanently as a result of the pandemic. Furthermore, 75.3% of small firms in Azerbaijan experienced a decrease in demand for their products and services compared to 59.6% of large firms and 58.2% of medium firms. SMEs also required a higher amount of government assistance: 65.5% of small firms and 67.6% of medium firms have received government assistance since the start of the pandemic. However, SMEs were more resilient to lay-offs (or did not have such flexibility): 58.8% of large firms in Azerbaijan reduced employment during the pandemic, compared to 29% of small firms and 22.9% of medium firms (see Figure 3).

Figure 3. Impact of COVID-19 pandemic on firms in Azerbaijan

% of firms in Azerbaijan

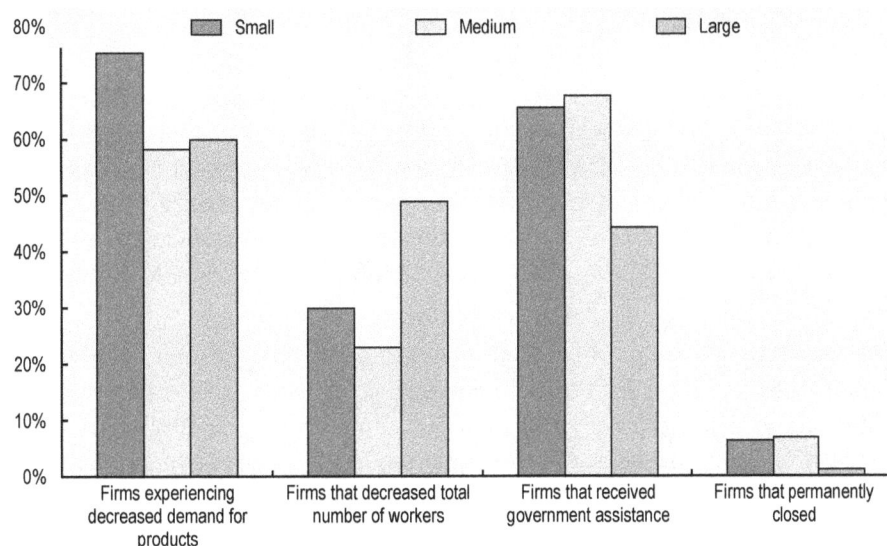

Source: (World Bank, 2021[3]).

In order to support households and businesses through the duration of COVID-19 related restrictions, Azerbaijan introduced a substantial economic support package, amounting to 4% of its GDP. The package was tailored to help businesses that were hit hardest by the pandemic, such as tourism, and included measures such as tax breaks for businesses, support for mortgage borrowers and transit companies, and assistance with utility payments. Under the package, businesses were able to apply for state guarantees of 60% of the loan amount and up to 50% interest rate subsidies for one year. Individual entrepreneurs and business owners also received financial assistance from the government. Social support programmes were also introduced, supporting citizens and helping to protect jobs and wages. The government delivered payments to over 600 000 low-income individuals in the spring and summer 2020, as well as providing unemployment insurance and food assistance to over 20 000 individuals (OECD, 2020[2]).

The economy continues to rely heavily on extractive industries

Azerbaijan's energy sector continues to drive its economy. Despite efforts to diversify production, employment and exports, the oil and gas sector generated around 38.2% of GDP in 2019 (State Statistical Committee of Azerbaijan, 2020[5]). Their indirect contribution to GDP is also tremendous, via demand for services and other activities dependent on the hydrocarbon sector's dynamics; thus, some estimates place the direct and indirect contribution of the sector to total GDP as high as 60% (International Fund for Agricultural Development, 2019[6]). Other sectors, such as agriculture and manufacturing make considerably smaller contributions and in 2020 they accounted for 6.9% and 5.8% of GDP, respectively (State Statistical Committee of Azerbaijan, 2020[5]).

Azerbaijan also continues to rely on its energy sector for exports, with hydrocarbons accounting for over 90% of all exports (Economist Intelligence Unit, 2021[7]). Primary export destinations are Italy, Turkey, Israel, India and Germany. For imports, Azerbaijan's key trading partners are Russia, Turkey, China, Switzerland and the United States (World Bank, 2019[8]). In 2020, as a consequence of global energy trade shocks, exports contracted by 11.5%. As COVID-19 restrictions gradually lifted in the first part of 2021, foreign trade recovered, with energy exports bouncing back. Imports also grew by 34% in early 2021, as domestic demand picked up with the lifting of COVID-19 lockdown measures (Economist Intelligence Unit, 2021[7]).

Despite important policy initiatives, the SME sector remains underdeveloped

SMEs in Azerbaijan are an important source of employment, but their full potential remains untapped. In 2019, Azerbaijan's SMEs generated 43.7% of total employment but only 14.9% of gross value added (see Figure 4). By way of comparison, SMEs in OECD countries account for about 60% of value added and 60-70% of employment. In part, this structure is a natural by-product of Azerbaijan's specialisation in capital-intensive extractive sectors, but its SMEs are largely concentrated in low-value added sectors – trade and repair of vehicles, transport and storage, and food service activities (State Statistical Committee of Azerbaijan, 2020[5]).

The Ministry of Economy is in charge of the SME policy agenda in Azerbaijan. It oversees the regulatory framework for enterprises and is responsible for creating a stimulating business environment. The Ministry oversees the State Service for Antimonopoly and Consumer Market Control as well as the State Tax Service. The Ministry of Economy also oversees important parts of business support infrastructure such as the Small and Medium Business Development Agency, which provides mostly non-financial support services for SMEs, and the Entrepreneurship Development Fund, which has a mandate to facilitate access to finance for SMEs.

Figure 4. Contribution of SMEs to Azerbaijan's economy (2019)

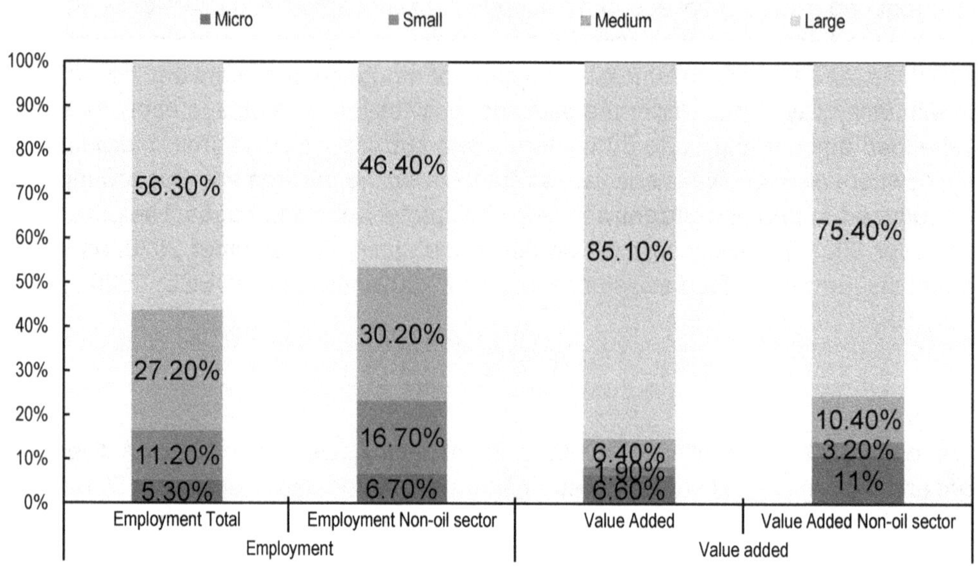

Note: According to the government's definition, micro enterprises have fewer than 10 employees and less than AZN 200 000 turnover; small enterprises have 10-49 employees and a turnover of less than AZN 3 000 000, and medium enterprises have 50-249 employees and a turnover of less than AZN 30 000 000.
Source: State Statistical Committee of Azerbaijan, database.

During the past five years, Azerbaijan has made significant progress in improving its business environment and fostering SME development. In 2015, the government launched a plan to enable a transition to a more diversified economy by adopting 12 *Strategic Roadmaps for the National Economy and Main Economic Sectors*, detailing goals for a number of economic policy reforms, including the development of the SME sector. As part of its *Strategic Roadmap for the Production of Consumer Goods at the Level of Small and*

Medium Enterprises in the Republic of Azerbaijan 2016-2020 (SME Roadmap), the government streamlined administrative procedures, expanded e-government services and launched a number of policy initiatives to stimulate private sector growth. The government also introduced tax exemptions for start-ups and individual entrepreneurs. It also introduced a new SME definition in December 2018, distinguishing between micro, small, medium and large enterprises (OECD, 2019[9]).

In the 2020 edition of the OECD SME Policy Index for Eastern Partner countries, Azerbaijan improved on 11 of 12 policy dimensions assessed, demonstrating a strong performance and high scores on operational environment (4.2), institutional and regulatory framework (3.53), and entrepreneurial learning/women's entrepreneurship (3.41). The main areas recommended for further improvement were innovation policy (2.83), SME skills (2.62), and green economy (2.31) (OECD et al., 2020[10]) (see Figure 5).

Figure 5. SBA Assessment score for Azerbaijan (2020)

Country scores by dimension 2020 vs. 2016

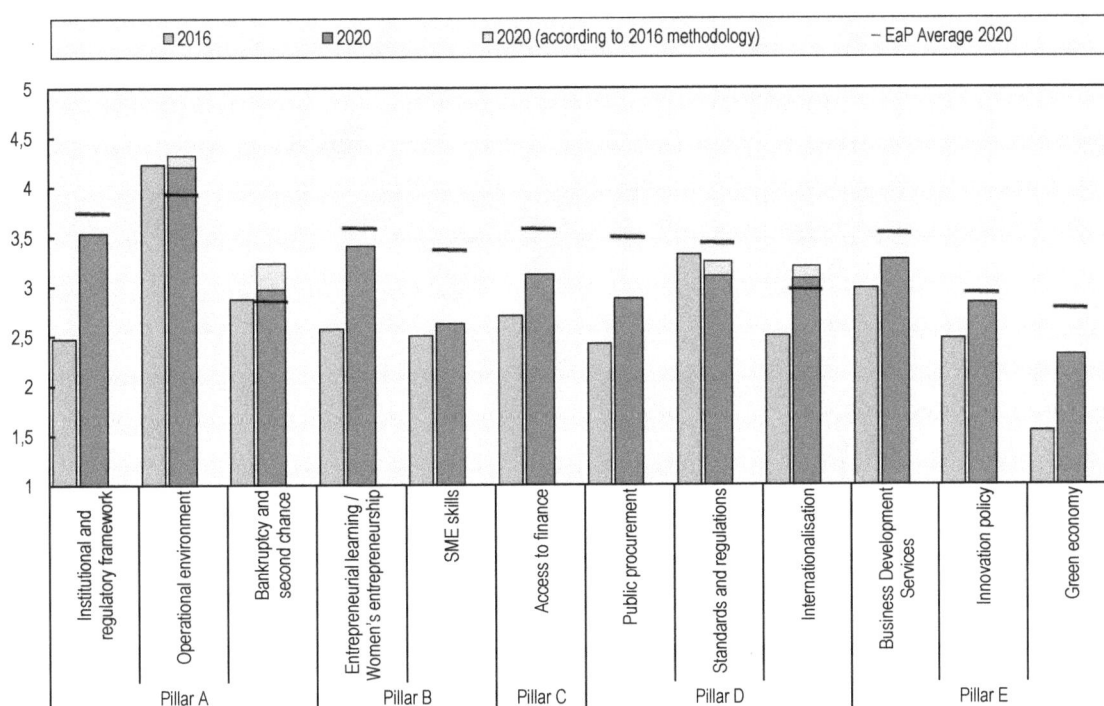

Source: (OECD et al., 2020[10]).

Azerbaijan could further improve the business environment by prioritising enforcement of competition rules to create level-playing-field conditions for all businesses, implementing measures to promote alternative dispute resolution and strengthening private-to-public litigation. Further efforts are also needed to improve the institutional and regulatory framework for SME policy, by improving co-ordination, strengthening public-private dialogue and ensuring that institutions responsible for SME development have appropriate resources to provide tailored services for SMEs. The government should also build on the skills intelligence approach using data collection instruments to target the needs of specific groups and sectors. The government will need to improve SME access to finance by supporting uptake of alternative sources of financing and fin-tech and making an effort to extend financial services to smaller enterprises, especially ones in rural areas (OECD et al., 2020[10]).

Putting digitalisation at the centre of SME policy making

Digital solutions can boost SME performance

Digitalisation can be broadly defined as the use of digital solutions and data with the objective to improve business operations, create revenue, transform business processes (not simply digitise them) and create an environment in which data and digital information are in its centre (Peillon and Dubruc, 2019[11]). It has the potential to boost SME development as it increases companies' ability to reach new markets, optimise and improve their operations, change the way how they engage with their employees. It can help them integrate more easily into global value chains, increase their innovation activity and boost productivity (OECD, 2019[12]). In particular, digitalisation can improve SME competitiveness via the following channels (OECD, 2021[13]):

- **Digitalisation enables SMEs to more easily access strategic resources**. Smaller businesses can leverage a wide range of digital instruments to finance their operations, such as peer-to-peer lending, crowdfunding, and initial coin offerings. SMEs with limited human resource management capabilities access a broader network of job-seekers that meet the desired skills profile.
- **Digital technologies help SMEs reach a wider customer base and integrate more easily in global markets**. Companies' websites and online e-commerce platforms make it possible to advertise and sell their products to a global audience. Furthermore, digitalisation reduces the costs associated with transport and border operations and makes a wide range of services tradeable.
- **Digitalisation allows SMEs to achieve scale without mass**. Digitalisation of products and services allows SMEs to develop successful digital products and increase their customer bases, revenues and productivity, while significantly bringing down their marginal costs (scale).
- **Digital platforms enable SMEs to capitalize on network effects**. OECD research has shown how digital platforms can deliver positive network effects to SMEs outsourcing business functions, such as advertising, e-commerce and service delivery to online platforms (OECD, 2019[14]).

Digitalisation is multi-faceted and often involves the use of application and digital tools and technologies to solve specific problems and improve operations implemented by businesses. Table 2 describes the most common digital solutions adopted by SMEs.

Digitalisation can also improve company performance: businesses decide to invest in digital tools and practices for a variety of reasons, and ultimately the process of technology adoption should bring about tangible benefits for firms undergoing digital transformation. Digitalisation can fuel productivity growth, which in turn brings wage growth, improvements in living standards and more digitalisation. Adoption of digital technologies has the potential to improve SME performance across all sectors, enhance firm productivity and lift living standards.

The COVID-19 pandemic created an unprecedented need to accelerate SME digitalisation as unprecedented quarantine measures highlighted both the limitations of non-digital business models and the opportunity gap between digitalised firms and those who lacked digital profiles.

Table 2. Selected digital solutions often adopted by SMEs

Technology	Description	Selected examples of application
High-speed broadband	Defined as having download speed of at least 100Mbit/s (i.e. fibre).	Adequate network access is essential to fully exploit exiting services over the internet and foster the diffusion of new ones.
Customer-Relations Management (CRM)	Used for managing a company's interactions with its customers and potential customers.	Coordination platforms: stakeholders can be put in direct contact and are constantly updated about the project's progression.
Cloud Computing (CC)	ICT services accessed over the internet, including services, storage, network components, and software applications.	Cloud Accounting: multiple users can simultaneously update information which allows to fasten the process and accessibility.
Supply-Chain Management (SCM)	Used for managing the flow of goods and services and concerns processes that transform raw materials into final products.	Supervisory Control and Data Acquisition (SCADA) Plant Management: integrated platform to monitor equipment and resources across the production line.
E-commerce	Describes the sale or purchase of goods or services conducted over computer networks by methods designed specifically for the purpose of receiving or placing orders. E-commerce can take place through a range of different commercial relationships, involving any possible pairing of customers, businesses or governments.	E-commerce platforms: they simplify the purchase process, increase product visibility and allow to reach a larger number of customers.
Enterprise Resource Planning (ERP)	Used to enhance back-office efficiency and strategic planning. These are software-based tools used for managing and integrating internal and external information flows.	Asset Inventory Management: allows to monitor inventories, thereby limiting the risk of overproduction and waste.
Radio Frequency Identification (RFID)	Allow near-field communication and are used for product identification, person identification or access control, monitoring and control of industrial production, supply chain inventory tracking and tracing, service maintenance information management, or payment applications.	Warehouse Management: tracking of assets to reduce the risk of loss and increase efficiency in shipment.
5G	5G technologies are expected to support applications such as smart homes and buildings, smart cities, 3D video, work and play in the cloud, remote medical services, virtual and augmented reality, and massive machine-to-machine communications for industry automation.	Virtual Reality for Simulation: they allow to visualise finalised product, allowing to improve training and ease the design. Although they are already being used, 5G will make the experience more realistic and effective, prompting an increase in diffusion and usage.
Blockchain	A shared ledger of transactions between parties in a network, not controlled by a single central authority.	Blockchain for Trade Documentation: end-to-end exchange of documents enabled by blockchain, increasing transaction security and transparency among all stakeholders.
Internet of Things (IoT)	Refers to the rapidly growing network of connected objects that are able to collect and exchange data in real time.	Traffic monitoring: useful in the management of vehicle traffic in large cities.
Artificial Intelligence (AI)	Simulation of human intelligence processes by computers.	Efficient Energy Management: digital sensors to monitor energy consumption, which allow to predict energy needs and reduce waste and costs.

Source: (OECD, 2019[15]); (OECD, 2019[16]); (ITU, 2019[17]).

Companies from different sectors can benefit from using these technologies at various stages of their digitalisation journey, ranging from the basic level of digitalisation to medium and advanced. Box 1 provides an example on how a company in the food manufacturing sector would apply digital solutions to improve its operations, optimise resources and ultimately increase efficiency.

Box 1. Example: Stages of Adopting Digital Solutions by the Food Manufacturing Sector

Selected digital solutions can be used on different stages of company development

Stage 1

During the first stage of digitalisation, the focus is on streamlining operations and optimising resources by automating labour-intensive tasks to improve productivity. At this stage, Enterprise Resource Planning (ERP) can be used for implementing solutions such as quality assurance, inventory management, fleet management, sales/order management and workforce management. Cloud Computing (CC) can also be used for inventory and fleet management, and sales/order management. The benefits of using ERP and CC at this stage are optimisation of features such as storage space and conditions, elimination of human errors, improving productivity or quality of food products, reducing inventory costs, more efficient tracking and management of sales to capture new business opportunities, and more. Access to high-speed broadband is also essential at this stage in order to perform these operations.

Stage 2

At this stage, the focus is on integrating assets, scaling business reach and accessing new opportunities through integrated platforms and optimised operations. Supply-Chain Management (SCM) and ERP at this stage are useful for implementing digital solutions such as e-commerce, manufacturing analytics, manufacturing operations management, overall equipment effectiveness and product authentication. The benefits of using these technologies at this stage involve increased efficiency in identifying problems at source affecting the quality of food, providing demand forecast for products based on trend analysis, increased productivity and improved traceability and accountability, improving the performance of equipment and building brand confidence amongst customers.

Stage 3

In stage 3 of digitalisation of a company, Internet of Things (IoT) and Artificial Intelligence (AI) can be used for implementing augmented reality for training and inspection, supervisory control and data acquisition plant management, predictive maintenance using big data and autonomous robots. A company in the food manufacturing sector in the late-stage of its digitalisation journey would benefit from these solutions through improved supervisory monitoring and control across the production line, optimisation of resources and a reduction of cost through scheduled maintenance of equipment, increased productivity and improved safety standards, and more.

Note: Example based on the industry plan for the food manufacturing industry created by SMEs Go Digital Project of Singapore.
Source: (IMDA, 2021[18]).

Promoting SME digitalisation calls for policies promoting digital culture and technology adoption

Promoting proactive SME digitalisation involves addressing market failures that put small firms at a disadvantage and creating an environment that provides equal opportunities for growth for SMEs and large firms. In order to create better conditions for a digital economy, it is important to manage the barriers that hinder technology adoption and innovation by SMEs.

Promoting SME digitalisation calls for: i) measures creating favourable framework conditions, ii) policies addressing market failures that put small firms at a disadvantage, which are related to their size, and iii) promotion of a digital culture among businesses and the general population (see Figure 6).

Figure 6. Framework for supporting SME digital transformation in Azerbaijan

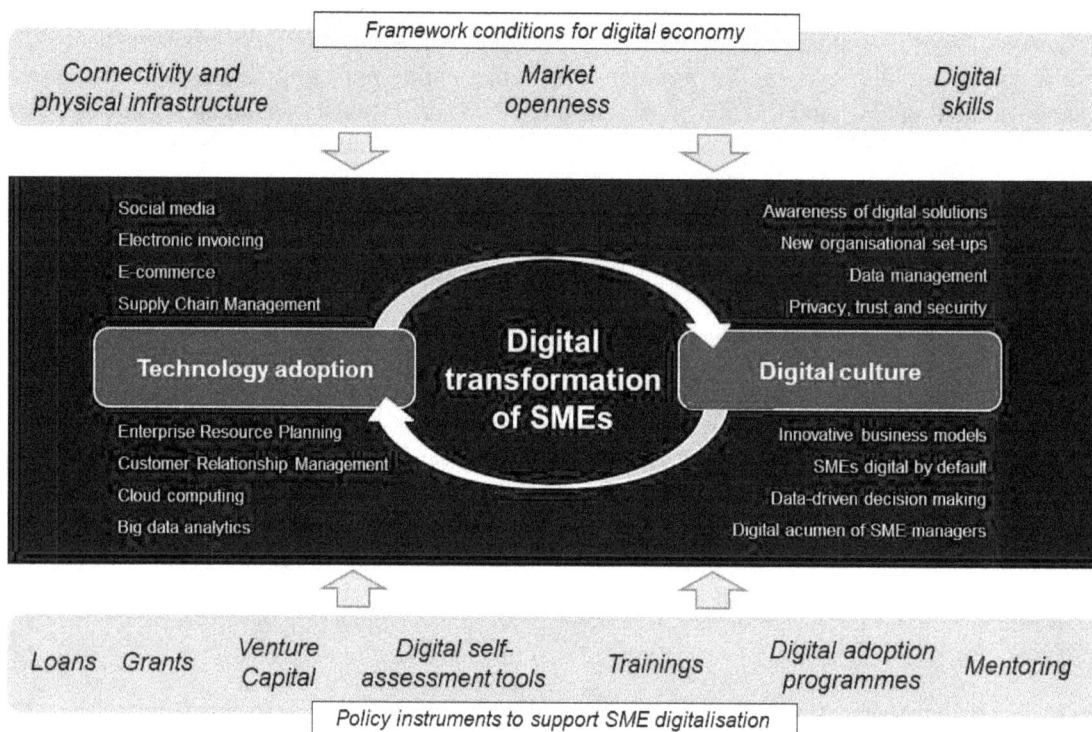

Source: OECD analysis.

Digitalisation is associated with risks related to security and digital divides

Despite its benefits, digital transformation is also associated with risks. SMEs that pursue digitalisation without implementing proper cybersecurity measures are vulnerable to digital security attacks. Digital security incidents have a wide range of causes, and can range from unintentional events such as human error, system bugs or other non-malicious causes, to malicious external actors engineering methods of attack on companies' digital systems. The COVID-19 crisis, which drove a lot of firms to move their operations online, also provided an opportunity for hackers to intensify attacks. Despite having lower "attack surfaces" – a lower volume and value of data to hack – when SMEs fall prey to cyberattacks, costs can be disproportionately large in terms of revenue. SMEs also tend to have lower investment in cybersecurity systems, often due to lack of funds. Furthermore, traditionally, smaller firms have a tendency to rely less on dedicated employees for carrying out ICT security-related activities compared to larger firms, largely due to less financial resources that could be dedicated to hiring security specialists (OECD, 2021[19]). These conditions make it particularly important for SMEs to pursue their digitalisation policies in tandem with investing in strong cybersecurity measures.

Another risk associated with digitalisation is the growing digital divide between firms that accelerate the development of their digital culture and those that do not. With broadband connection being a pre-requisite for businesses to be a part of the digital community, firms that are less connected (for instance, those that do not have access to the internet) fall behind better-connected competitors. Given that a sizeable number of firms in Azerbaijan do not have an online presence or access to the internet, blanket policies for digitalisation of firms put smaller firms with less financial capacity at risk of losing customers and falling out of the market. With the growing reliance on e-commerce and online platforms for business operations, there is a growing concern that the push for digitalisation can be disruptive, leading to a more polarised economy and an uneven playing field, with large firms reaping the benefits (EIB, 2020[20]).

Digitalisation is among Azerbaijan's policy priorities

In 2015, Azerbaijan has launched 12 Strategic Roadmaps to ensure economic diversification and sustainable economic growth. Digital transformation of the economy was embedded in this strategic reform agenda and a number of related reforms were implemented between 2016 and 2020. Digitalisation was covered under the Strategic Roadmap for Development of Telecommunications and Information Technologies (ICT Roadmap) and the Strategic Roadmap for the Production of Consumer Goods at the Level of Small and Medium Enterprises in the Republic of Azerbaijan (SME Roadmap).

The ICT Roadmap, which was implemented under the supervision of the Ministry of Digital Development and Transport (MDDT), identified three strategic targets and 10 policy priorities aimed at improving governance, supporting productivity growth and digitising government services (see Table 3).

Table 3. Strategic targets and policy priorities of Azerbaijan's ICT Roadmap 2016-2020

Strategic target	Policy priority
1. Improve governance structures, and strengthen ICT	1.1. Establish an independent regulatory body
	1.2. Liberalise the telecommunication market
	1.3. Increase mobile infrastructure investments
2. Increase productivity and operational efficiency of the business environment	2.1. Extend digital payments and apply ICT in education system
	2.2 Extend technology-based operations in business environment
	2.3. Upgrade technology education with the involvement of businesses
	2.4. Improve the electronic systems of government institutions
	2.5. Increase knowledge and skills in the ICT sector
3. Digitise government and social environment	3. 1. Improve the information systems of government institutions
	3. 2 Create an end-to-end integrated e-health infrastructure

Source: Government of Azerbaijan (2016), *Strategic Roadmap for Development of Telecommunications and Information Technologies*, https://monitoring.az/assets/upload/files/6683729684f8895c1668803607932190.pdf.

In addition to the ICT Roadmap, there are a number of measures under the SME Roadmap aimed at boosting the digital transformation of Azerbaijan's economy, and its SME sector in particular. For example, SMBDA provides SMEs with financial and non-financial support including in the area of SME digitalisation. Policy initiatives to support SME access to finance, such as the Entrepreneurship Development Fund and Mortgage and Credit Guarantee Fund, can ease SME access to digital technologies and provide SMEs with financial resources needed to undergo digital transformation. Moreover, business incubators can help build digital awareness and boost abilities of entrepreneurs to implement digital solutions.

The digital transformation is also envisaged by *Azerbaijan 2030: National Priorities for Socio-Economic Development*, a strategic policy document approved in February 2021. The document identifies 5 priorities: i) Sustainable growth and competitive economy, ii) Society based on inclusive and social justice, iii) Competitive human capital and innovations, iv) Stronger development of Azerbaijan's territories and, v) Clean environment and green growth. The document outlines the overall vision and should be followed by a set of five-year strategy documents and policy action plans, which should detail policy objectives and actions across different policy areas. It is expected that digitalisation of the public and the private sector will be high on the reform agenda and planned SME development strategy 2021-2025 will define a set of policy intervention to promote uptake of digital technologies among SMEs and general population.[2]

Adoption of digital technologies by SMEs in Azerbaijan remains limited

Limited access of Azerbaijan's enterprises to computers and the internet continues to limit their ability to benefit from digital solutions. For example, while the share of enterprises with internet access increased significantly in the last decade, only 51.5% of enterprises in Azerbaijan were using the internet in 2019, compared to 13.8% in 2009 (see Figure 7). Despite the significant progress, Azerbaijan still lags behind regional peers and OECD countries. For example, 90% of companies from Belarus and Ukraine reported access to the internet, as do almost 100% of companies from the OECD area (The State Statistical Committee of the Republic of Azerbaijan, 2019[21]) (OECD, 2021[13]).

Figure 7. Internet and computer usage in Azerbaijan, 2019

% of total

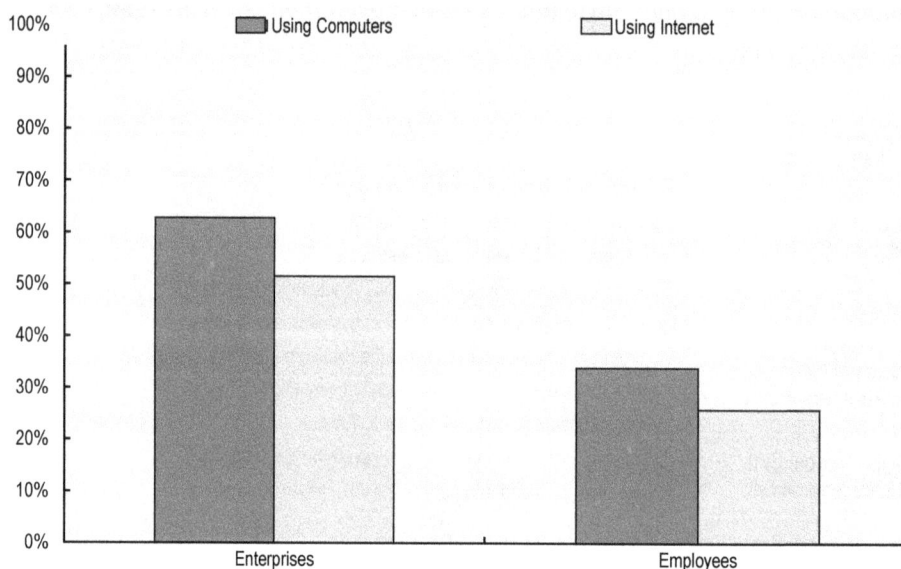

Source: (The State Statistical Committee of the Republic of Azerbaijan, 2019[21]).

---

[2] Digitalisation is also embedded in a number of presidential decrees and orders, such as 1) on "Improvement of management in the field of digital transformation"; 2) on "Improvement of management in the field of digitalization, innovation, high technologies and communication"; 3) on "approval of State Programme on enhancement of digital payments in the Republic of Azerbaijan in 2018-2020 years".

Despite the lack of official data on the adoption of digital solutions by SMEs, the available evidence suggests that Azerbaijan's SMEs are not taking advantage of available digital technologies and are lagging behind in adopting digital solutions. For example, only 9.8% of enterprises in Azerbaijan have a website compared to the average of 76.7% in OECD countries (The State Statistical Committee of the Republic of Azerbaijan, 2019[21]). A survey implemented by United States Agency for International Development (USAID) with companies operating in agriculture and tourism from Azerbaijan, Ukraine, Georgia and Belarus found that a majority of companies in this sector did not adopt digital solutions to make their operations more efficient and bring their products closer to customers (USAID, 2021[22]). Azerbaijan also lags behind its regional peers in utilisation of internet activities by individuals. Specifically, Azerbaijan has a particularly low share of population that uses internet banking, finds information about goods or services, purchases goods or services online (see Figure 8).

Figure 8. Internet activities undertaken by individuals

% of population, 2018 or latest year available

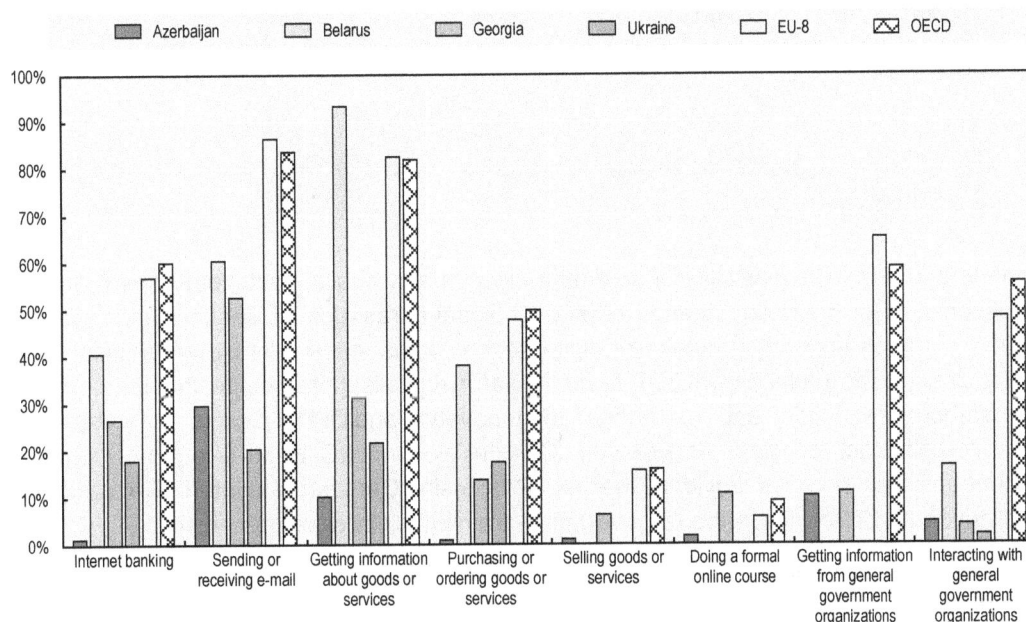

Source: ITU.

According to the World Bank's enterprise surveys, the pandemic has accelerated the use of digital tools for companies of all sizes in Azerbaijan. More than 60% of small and 70% of medium-sized enterprises in Azerbaijan have increased their online activity (see Figure 9). Some of these changes are going to become irrevocable, as SMEs that experienced the benefits of going digital are unlikely to (fully) return to a brick-and-mortar model once the pandemic is over (OECD, 2021[13]).

Figure 9. % of firms that started or increased online business activity in response to COVID-19

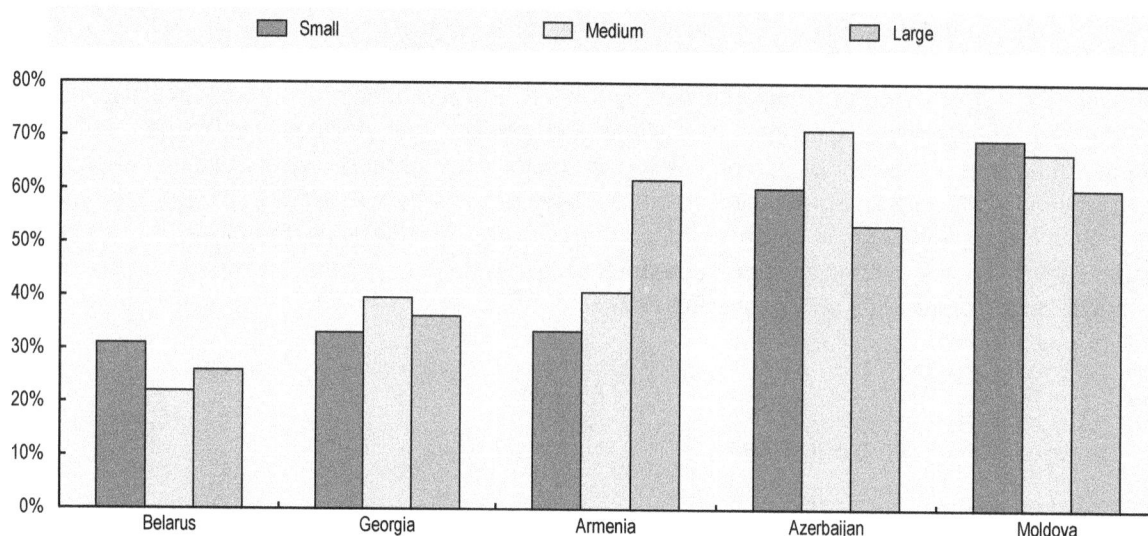

Source: (World Bank, 2021[3]).

Digitalisation policy agenda is distributed among different institutions with limited co-ordination

Digitalisation is under the responsibility of several ministries and public institutions (see Figure 10). The MDDT is responsible for the policy agenda related to digital infrastructure, security and regulation, and also oversees initiatives supporting uptake of digital technologies, especially by companies operating in the IT sector. Institutions under the MDDT responsiblefor digitalisation include the Electronic Security Service (cybersecurity education and awareness), the Innovation and Digital Development Agency (uptake and adoption of digital technologies), Aztelekom LLC, AzInTelecom LLC, Baku Telephone Communication LLC (telecommunication services provider), the Data Processing Centre (e-signature, SmartPay systems), an ICT Application and Training Centre (e-governance training, skills development).

The Ministry of Economy is responsible for the policy agenda related to SME development and economic diversification. It oversees the Small and Medium Businesses Development Agency (business development services), the Entrepreneurship Development Fund (financial support), and the 4th Industrial Revolution Centre (awareness and information support).

Azerbaijani Service and Assessment Network (ASAN) and ASAN Support for Family Business (ABAD) operating under the State Agency for Public Services and Social Innovations (SAPSSI) provide e-government services for SMEs and the general population and support development of family-run businesses located primarily in the rural areas of Azerbaijan. Established under the same agency, the Centre of Development of Electronic Government, as well as the Center of Innovations aim to improve electronic services, particularly those related to government-to-business (G2B) and business-to-government (B2G). The Center of Innovations provides in particular also services to start-ups and co-working services through its "Innoland" Incubation and Acceleration Center.

The Ministry of Education is responsible for embedding digitalisation in the curriculum and implementing programmes to support digital literacy among the wider population. During the COVID-19 pandemic, the Ministry of Education quickly shifted to online education. However, many students, especially those from rural areas or from low-income families did not have access to online education during the lockdowns.

Figure 10. Public institutions responsible for digitalisation agenda in Azerbaijan

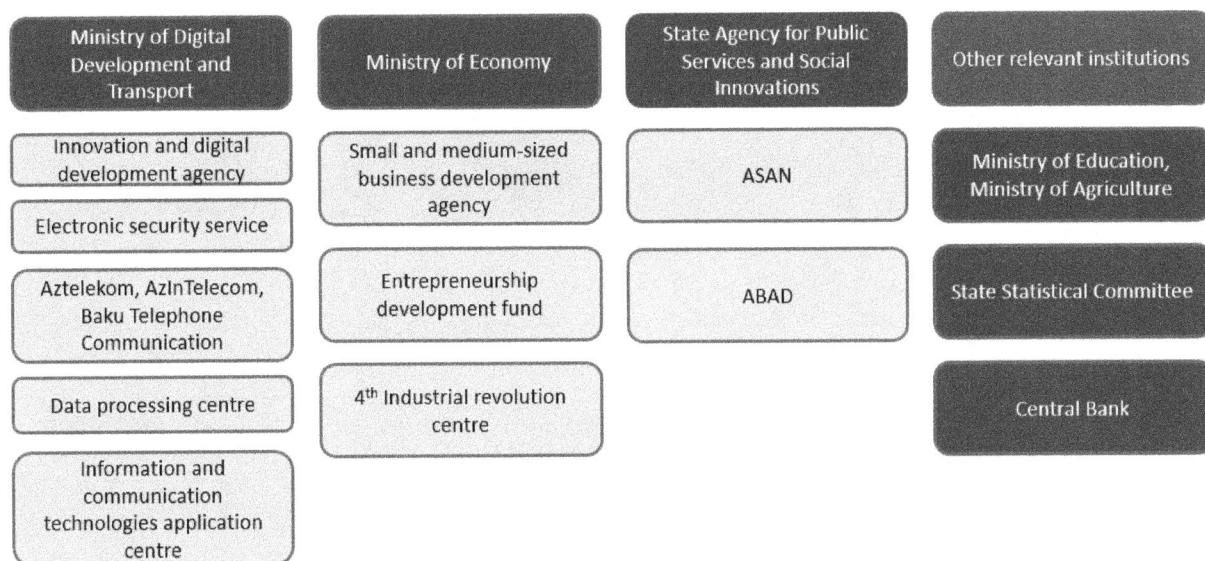

Ministry of Digital Development and Transport	Ministry of Economy	State Agency for Public Services and Social Innovations	Other relevant institutions
Innovation and digital development agency	Small and medium-sized business development agency	ASAN	Ministry of Education, Ministry of Agriculture
Electronic security service			
Aztelekom, AzInTelecom, Baku Telephone Communication	Entrepreneurship development fund	ABAD	State Statistical Committee
Data processing centre	4th Industrial revolution centre		Central Bank
Information and communication technologies application centre			

Source: OECD authors based on the Project Working Group meetings.

Overall, the digitalisation policy agenda in Azerbaijan remains fragmented, spread across legal and strategic documents and public institutions with limited co-ordination. This can be partially explained by the complexity of that agenda, which cannot be clearly associated with one policy initiative or institution and is rather multi-dimensional. However, a number of institutions and initiatives have overlapping objectives and limited co-ordination/co-operation results in lower impact of their activities.

Creating framework conditions for SME digitalisation

Providing digital infrastructure and ensuring regulatory frameworks aligned with the latest global trends are crucial for the digital transformation of economies. Successful uptake of digital technologies by firms and households depends, in particular, on:

- **Digital infrastructure**: High-quality communications infrastructure is essential to embark on the digital transformation. Accessible, affordable and reliable internet connection is essential to enable people and companies to participate in the digital economy.

- **Regulatory framework**: Fostering digital transformation calls for a regulatory framework that will stimulate investment into digital infrastructure, ensure a safe digital environment (data privacy and cybersecurity), support e-commerce and provide digital platforms for government-to-business (G2B) and business-to-business (B2B) communication.

- **Digital skills:** Adequate digital skills amongst the population are essential to ensure that digital transformation benefits all and avoids exacerbating existing inequalities. Skills for digital transformation involve a range of foundational competences, including literacy, numeracy and problem-solving skills (OECD, 2020[23]).

Digital infrastructure in Azerbaijan has improved, but regional differences still exist

Digital infrastructure refers to technologies that provide the foundation for reliable connection and digital operations. Physical infrastructures such as data centres, fibre optic cables and mobile phone towers are essential for providing access to broadband connection (OECD, 2018[24]). The pandemic accelerated the demand for investing in online communities and digital infrastructure, placing connectivity high on the agenda for businesses whose operations were negatively affected by lockdowns. Gaps in digitalisation are particularly persistent between urban and rural areas, the latter of which in Azerbaijan have less digital infrastructure in place to allow for digital transformation.

Access to broadband internet in Azerbaijan improved over the last decade, increasing from 5.26 per 100 population in 2010 to 19.68 in 2020 (see Figure 11).

Figure 11. Evolution of broadband subscriptions in EaP countries

Broadband subscriptions per 100 population, 2010-2020

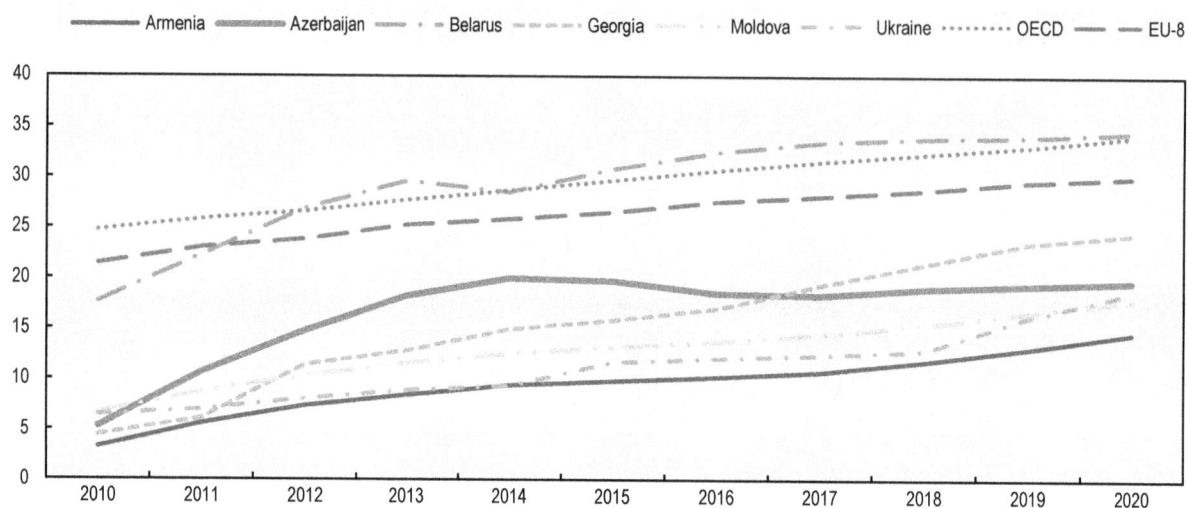

Source: (ITU, 2021[25]).
Note: Median values for OECD and EU-8 (Czech Republic, Estonia, Hungary, Latvia, Lithuania, Slovenia, Slovak Republic, Poland).

A discernible digital divide still exists in Azerbaijan, with different levels of broadband connectivity between rural and urban regions. These gaps can be attributed to shortages of required infrastructure, as well as lower levels of digital literacy and skills in rural areas of the country (Asian Development Bank, 2019[26]). In 2019, more than half of all enterprises in Baku had internet access, compared with as little as a third of enterprises in some rural regions (see Figure 12).

Figure 12. Evolution of enterprises with internet access in Azerbaijan by region (%)

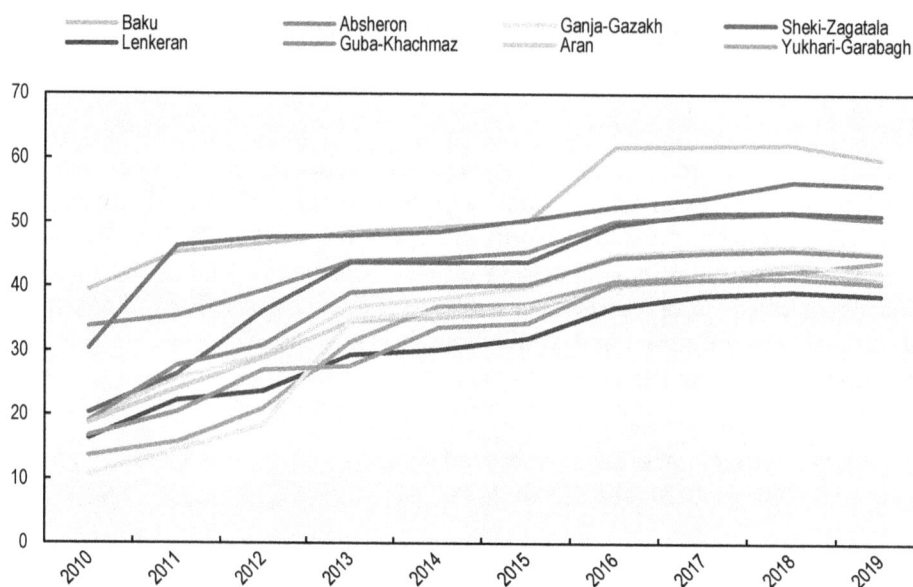

Source: (The State Statistical Committee of the Republic of Azerbaijan, 2019[21]).

Even though mobile broadband subscriptions have increased substantially over the last decade and 99% of households have access to mobile phones, Azerbaijan has only 70 mobile broadband subscriptions per 100 population, well below the OECD average (112) (see Figure 13).

Figure 13. Evolution of mobile broadband subscriptions in EaP countries

Mobile Broadband Subscriptions per 100 population, 2010-2020

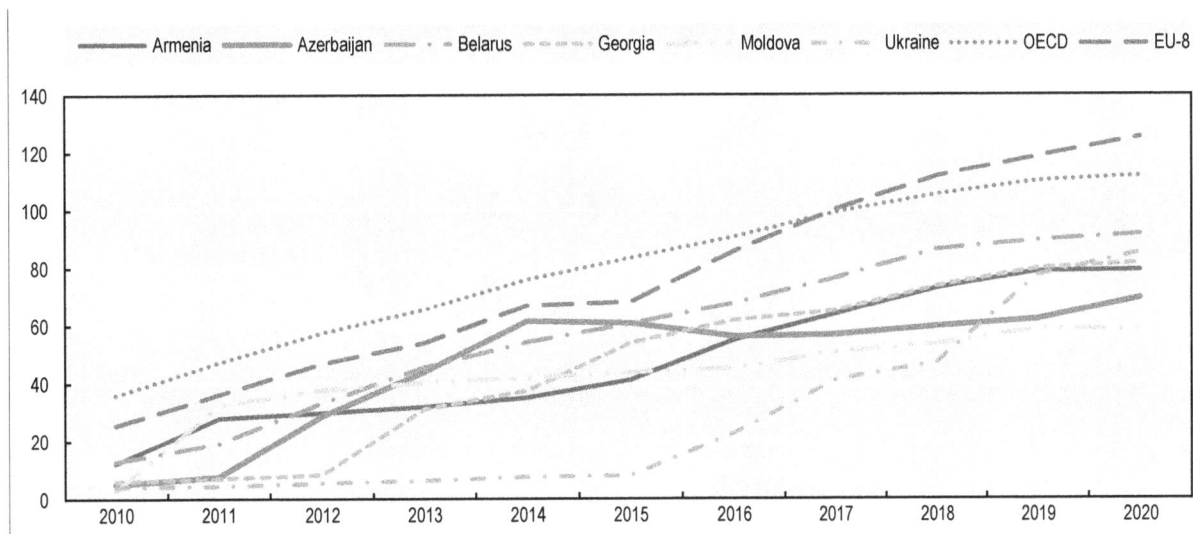

Note: Median values for OECD and EU-8 (Czech Republic, Estonia, Hungary, Latvia, Lithuania, Slovenia, Slovak Republic, Poland). Data are not available for Ukraine for 2019.
Source: (ITU, 2021[25]).

In 2017, the most recent year for which ICT Development Scores were published by International Telecommunications Union, Azerbaijan's ICT Development Index score was 6.2. It ranked third among EaP countries, behind Belarus and Moldova with ICT Development Index scores of 7.55 and 6.45, respectively. Azerbaijan's score breakdown shows that it lags behind in number of fixed-telephone subscriptions per 100 inhabitants (17.52) and fixed broadband subscriptions per 100 inhabitants (18.58) (see Figure 14).

Figure 14. Azerbaijan ICT Development Index (2017)

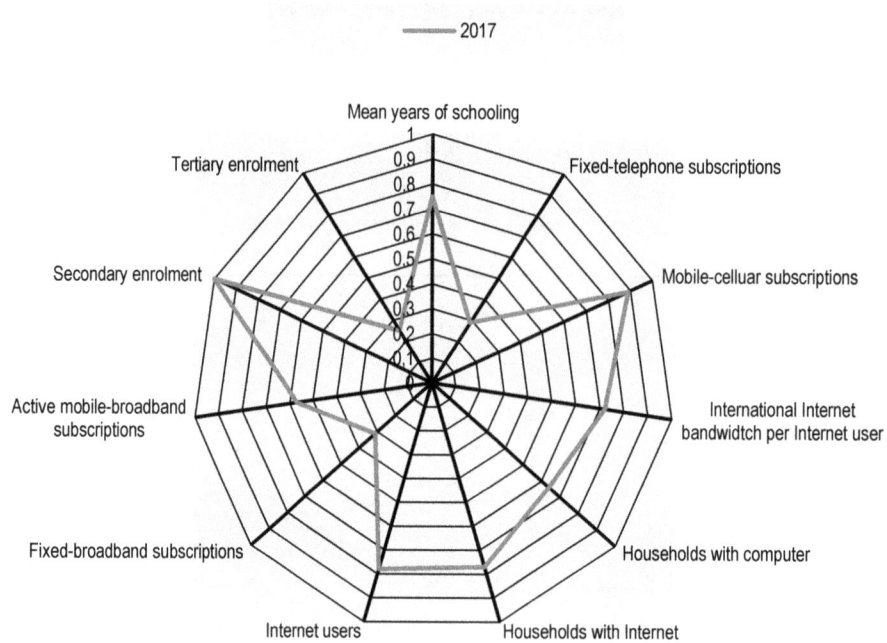

Source: (ITU, 2021[25]).

In terms of barriers to foreign direct investment (FDI) in telecommunications, Azerbaijan's score is lower than the OECD average on the OECD FDI Regulatory Restrictiveness Index, which means that, at least in terms of statutory restrictions, Azerbaijan is more open to FDI than the OECD average. There are few formal barriers to FDI in Azerbaijan, and market conditions are comparable with most open OECD economies.

An independent national regulatory body (NRA) for the telecommunications sector is important to promote objective and well-reasoned decision making, as well as to foster fair market competition, as a regulator's source of funding can influence its level of autonomy and create an uneven playing field. An independent NRA for telecommunications and ICTs usually obtains funding through legislative and budgetary allocations, which in turn allows for transparency in identifying budget requirements and allocating finances.

In October 2021, Azerbaijan established the Information and Communication Technologies Agency which acts as a national regulatory authority under the Ministry of Digital Development and Transport.[3] It is essential to ensure that the Regulatory Authority is independent, meaning it is not affected by political or market influence and obtains funding through legislative and budgetary allocations, which in turn allows for transparency in identifying budget requirements and allocating finances. It is also important for promoting market openness (ITU, 2020[27]).

---

[3] The Information and Communication Technologies Agency is a public legal entity that carries out certification, accounting, regulation and control in the field of information and communication technologies (including quality control), as well as regulation of interconnection between telecommunication operators and radio spectrum management.

Azerbaijan has reformed its regulatory framework for digitalisation, but significant gaps remain

Trust and security

Inadequate security measures can have far-reaching consequences for SME operations resulting in financial damage, loss of reputation and consumer trust (OECD, 2021[19]). The most common types of digital security threats include phishing, malware and ransomware (OECD, 2020[23]). Implementing digital security measures is crucial for protecting organisations and customers against cyberattacks.

Azerbaijan ranks 40th in the Global Cybersecurity Index 2020 published by the International Telecommunication Union. Its highest scores are for Legal Measures and Co-operative Measures, while its lowest is Organisational Measures (see Figure 15). Overall, Azerbaijan is the best performer among the EaP countries and ranks third in the CIS region (after Kazakhstan and Russian Federation) (ITU, 2021[25]).

Figure 15. Global Security Index scores for Azerbaijan, 2020

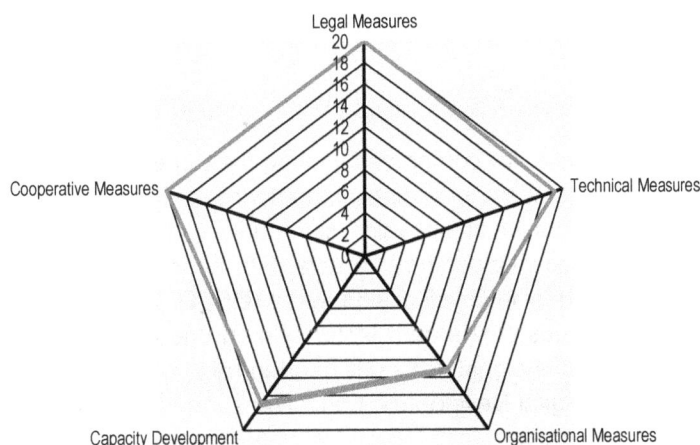

Source: ITU (2020), Global Cybersecurity Index 2020, https://www.itu.int/epublications/publication/global-cybersecurity-index-2020/en/.

Azerbaijan has not adopted a national cybersecurity strategy, but some policy objectives in this field are defined in the National Strategy on the Development of the Information Society (2014 -2020) as well as in the ICT Roadmap (2016-2020). Currently, there is not any strategic policy document in place that would define mid-term policy priorities in the area of cybersecurity. The preparation of the National Strategy on information Security and Cyber security for 2022-2027 years is ongoing.[4]

In 2012, the Electronic Security Service (ESS) was established under the Ministry of Digital Development and Transport as the main public entity responsible for policy co-ordination, awareness raising and prevention of cyberattacks. The ESS co-ordinates the activities of information infrastructure entities in the field of cyber security, takes measures in cases of illegal collection, processing and non-protection of personal data, informs the country about current and potential electronic threats, educates public, private

---

[4] In September 2009, Azerbaijan signed the Convention on Cybercrime, also known as the Budapest Convention. The Budapest Convention is a framework that permits practitioners from the Parties to share experience and create relationships that facilitate cooperation.

and other organizations in the field of cyber security and provides them with methodological assistance. It also collects and analyses information from users, software and hardware producers, notifies about the cybersecurity risks, implements preventive measures and provides recommendations and instructions.

The Computer Emergency Response Centre under the Special Communication and Information Security State Service of the Republic of Azerbaijan plays an important role in the fight against cyber threats. It gathers information about cyberattacks and renders assistance to public and private sector to prevent them. The Centre also provides information support about existing cyber risks.

In terms of programmes to promote digital security, most activities are related to the organisation of public events and workshops. For example, the annual International Cyber Security Week organised by the Ministry of Digital Development and Transport aims at creating a platform to promote implementation of digital security measures by companies and public sector entities, increasing digital security awareness, creating appropriate methodological tools to implement cyber-security measures and improving co-ordination between the private and public sectors in this field (Azintelecom, 2020[28]). In 2015, the Ministry established the Cyber Academy – an initiative promoting cyber-security awareness and skills among companies, workers and the general population. There are also a number of private sector initiatives aiming to build awareness and foster implementation of digital security measures. However, public institutions do not currently implement comprehensive programmes that would provide SMEs with the tools and skills required to effectively face cybersecurity challenges as existing initiatives are either one-off or low-scale and do not have the ability to reach a critical mass of SMEs.

E-signature

Electronic signatures are essential for companies moving their operations online, allowing them to meet the legal and contractual requirements for maintaining integrity online without paperwork. Examples of e-signatures include simple photocopies or a physical signature, or more complex structures such as verified signatures, which use mathematical algorithms to establish the identity of the signatory. Functionally, e-signatures are recognised as equal to physical signatures (OECD, 2021[13]). The e-signature is a valuable digital tool for businesses and customers, and is considered one of the main attributes of a successful digital transformation. The use of e-signatures goes hand-in-hand with a robustly developed digital culture. In Azerbaijan, the Ministry of Digital Development and Transport is responsible for the implementation of e-signatures (E-Gov, 2021[29]).

In 2004, the government passed the Law on Digital Electronic Signature which required e-signatures in Azerbaijan to be certified by an organisation approved by the Ministry Digital Development and Transport. However, there are many challenges with certifications due to the low level of e-commerce penetration in the country. There is also low interest in innovative financial technologies, such as blockchain and cryptocurrencies. Digital identification exists based on SIM cards, which have become very useful for identifying those who access online government services (Asian Development Bank, 2019[26]).

In 2011, the National Certificate Services Centre of the Ministry of Digital Development and Transport was launched with the purpose to provide services to citizens, legal entities, entrepreneurs and civil servants. Registration centres were organised in major central post offices and branches in Baku city, and post offices in the country's regions as well as through the E-İmza website (http://e-imza.az/).

Between 2011 and 2020, a total of 245 848 e-signature certificates were issued through the centre, to citizens, government agencies and legal entities. The majority of certificates were issued to government entities, while private citizens made up the smallest percentage of those having received e-signature certificates, indicating limited use of e-signature among entrepreneurs and the general population (National Certification Services Centre, 2018[30]).[5]

In addition, citizens are able to use Asan İmza (Mobile ID), which is a mobile identity card that can be used when using electronic services and digital signature verification. Asan İmza works as a SIM card for mobile phones and contains electronic certificates similar in function to identification cards, allowing users to perform all online activities. In order to use the service, citizens have to buy a special SIM card and use their mobile ID on a compatible website, or other devices for authentication and digital signature. The system is implemented according to Public Key Infrastructure (PKI) and launched by mobile operators in co-operation with the ASAN Certification Services Centre (ASXM).

E-commerce

E-commerce enables SMEs to expand their customer and supplier bases, thus providing access to new markets. This became particularly important during the COVID-19 pandemic, as e-commerce enabled SMEs to not only retain sales and revenue amidst lockdowns, but also to increase their customer bases, create economies of scale through network effects, and improve cost efficiency (OECD, 2021[19]).

E-commerce in Azerbaijan nevertheless remains underdeveloped: in 2017, only 5% of customers in Azerbaijan purchased something via the internet, compared to a world average of 24%. In 2016, retail e-commerce accounted for 0.04% of GDP. Despite almost doubling between 2016 and 2017 (from AZN 25.6 million to AZN 46 million), retail e-ecommerce is still low compared to neighbouring countries. The State Programme on Expansion of Digital Payments for 2018-2020 reported that the share of e-commerce in retail sales in 2018 was only 0.2% (Centre for Analysis on Economic Reforms and Communication, 2018[31]). Despite being in an early stage of development, e-commerce sales growth in the EaP is expected to surpass the European average, with Azerbaijan reaching 4.6% growth in 2022 (see Figure 16).

Figure 16. Size of e-commerce market in EaP countries

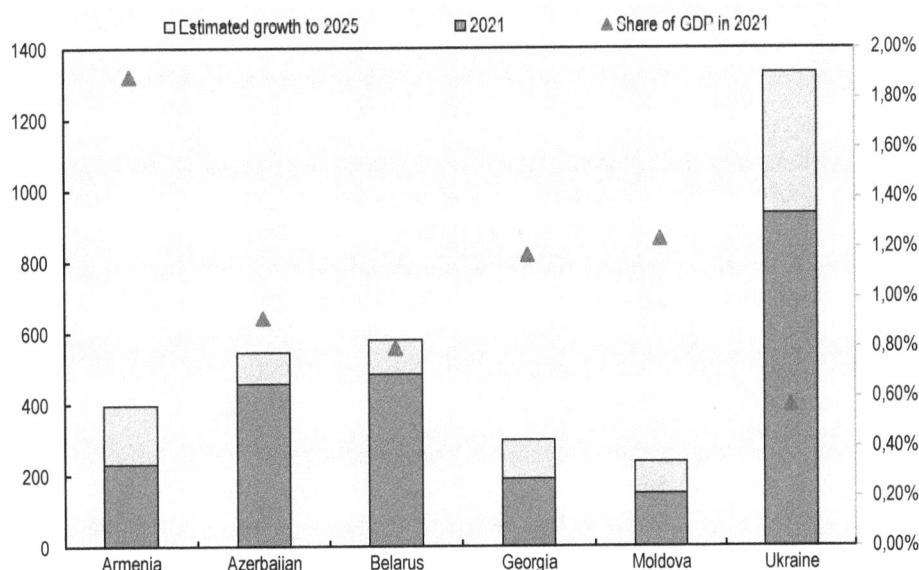

Source: OECD calculations based on e-commerce market size estimates from (Statista, 2021[32]). GDP estimates from (IMF, 2021[33]).

---

[5] In the framework of the new e-Government infrastructure of Azerbaijan, the "ASAN Login" system was developed, a Single Sign-On System created by the E-GOV Development Center (EGDC) to facilitate access to e-services provided by public and private organizations through one integrated portal.

Azerbaijan ranks 68th out of 144 countries on the business-to-consumer (B2C) e-commerce index. This low ranking reflects low penetration of e-payments, a shortage of domestic online shops, underdeveloped logistics, lack of trust by both buyers and sellers, low digital literacy, and high costs associated with international credit card payment networks (Asian Development Bank, 2019[26]).

Cash payments are still prevalent in Azerbaijan, and the lack of a digital banking culture prevents the development of e-commerce. For example, in 2017 less than 5% of population older than 15 years used internet to buy something online and less than 10% used internet to pay bills (see Figure 17).

Figure 17. Use of digital financial services in the EaP countries

% aged 15+ (2017)

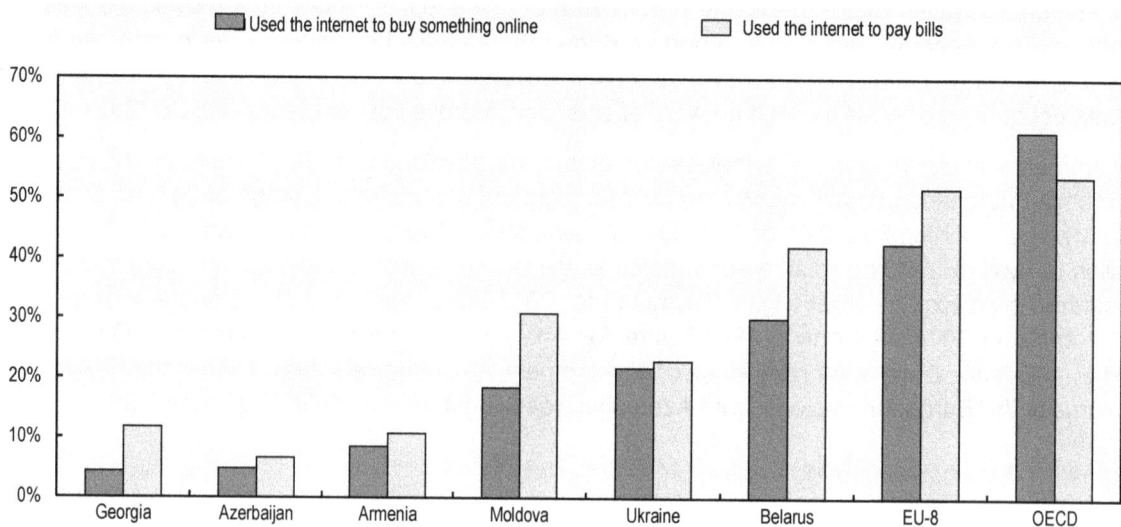

Source: (World Bank, 2017[34]).

When comparing the state of affairs on e-commerce in Azerbaijan vs. in the EU, some gaps in practices stand out. Most notably, global e-commerce marketplaces are not directly available in Azerbaijan, and the businesses and customers have a poorer awareness on how to use cross-border platforms and have low levels of digital skills. While businesses and customers from Azerbaijan buy and sell in the EU, poor digital literacy constitutes a barrier to using global marketplaces that are operating in the EU. Furthermore, there are gaps in payment methods usage. Digital wallets are not common in Azerbaijan, marketplaces do not use global payment gateways to process payments, and the digital platform PayPal is available in the country only to make payments to others, not to receive payments (EU4Digital, 2021[35]).

The Law on E-Commerce regulates all areas of e-commerce except the financial market, insurance and securities market. The Law on Electronic Signature and Electronic Document was first adopted in 2004 and last updated in 2018. Unlike EaP countries that have Association Agreements with the European Union (EU) (Moldova, Ukraine, Georgia) and are aligning their e-commerce legislation in line with EU standards, Azerbaijan does not have such requirements (EU4Digital, 2021[35]).

Azerbaijan started to implement a number of measures to support the uptake of e-commerce under the *State Programme on Expansion of Digital Payments in the Republic of Azerbaijan in 2018-2020*. For example, the central bank launched an instant payment system, which should improve access to online payment services and a new law on Law on Payment Services and Payment Systems is expected to create a sound legal framework (Central Bank of Azerbaijan, 2021[36]). In addition, measures were implemented to increase the potential of "Azerpost" (https://www.azerpost.az) for accurate and timely delivery of items purchased by customers from the internet by integration with worldwide sales networks such as Amazon and Alibaba, as well as world's leading transport and logistics companies such as DHL and TNT. In addition, under the Azexport platform (https://azexport.az/), Azerbaijan is developing cross-border digital trade through partnerships with some of the world's largest e-commerce companies. To conclude, the SMBDA has established an e-commerce platform (www.kobmarket.az) to support SMEs in making their prodicts known and available to a wider costumer base.

E-government services

Using digital platforms to provide e-government services provides unprecedented opportunity to simplify administrative and bureaucratic processes, improve public access to information on administrative requirements, reduce opportunities for corruption, and cut the time required to perform administrative functions. It can also provide SMEs with incentives to further technology adoption (OECD, 2020[37]).

The government has made significant progress in expanding e-government services. Improvements have been made allowing company registration, business licensing, public procurement, customs and visa application procedures to be completed online (OECD, 2019[38]). Azerbaijan's score on the United Nations (UN) E-Government Index increased in the last decade from 0.45 to 0.71 (see Figure 18). Across the three sub-categories of the E-Government Index – the online services index, the telecommunication infrastructure index and the human capital index – Azerbaijan achieved scores of 0.7, 0.65 and 0.77, respectively, in 2020, compared to 0.32, 0.13 and 0.91 in 2010. This indicates that while government's efforts to reform e-government services have brought improvements, more progress is required, especially in the area of human capital index, as the score for this particular subsection has declined since 2010 (UN, 2021[39]).

Figure 18. UN E-Government Development Index for EaP countries

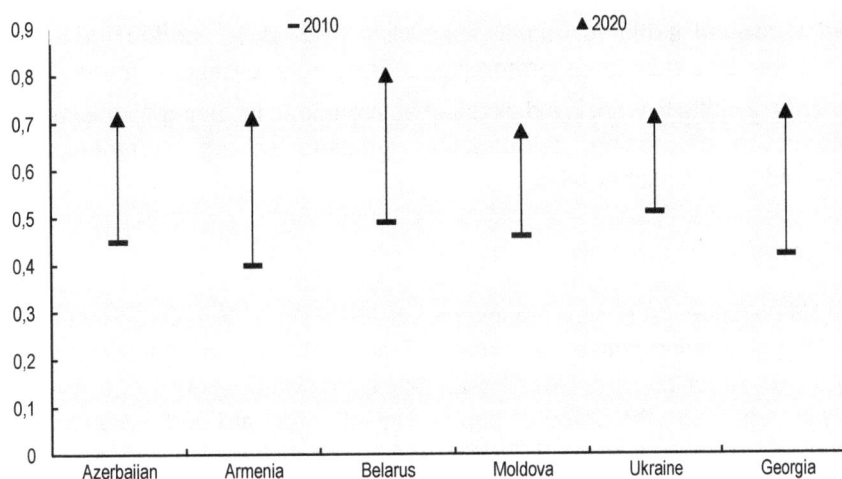

Note: The e-government development index incorporates access characteristics, such as the infrastructure and educational levels, to reflect how a country is using information technologies to promote access and inclusion of its people.
Source: (UN, 2021[39]).

In March 2018, Azerbaijan established an e-government portal (https://www.e-gov.az/) that provides access to over 500 government services for the general population and companies. These government services range in the areas of social protection, social security, education, health, communication, online payments, customs, legal, tax and other services. The portal was identified as best practice in the region by the World Bank, as it significantly expanded online services to SMEs (OECD, 2019[38]). However, like other EaP countries, Azerbaijan has not yet reached the high level of inter-operability required to transition to full digitalisation, meaning there is not enough information exchange between different digitalised services (OECD, 2020[37]).

The e-SMB House Portal (https://e-smb.gov.az/) is an electronic system operating as part of the SMBDA. The Portal is a unified platform of SME houses, and is a valuable tool for SMEs to access public electronic services and maintain their accounting records. The Portal can be used to pay customs duties, and make payments for services and G2B services. Finally, via the Portal, entrepreneurs are able to use various financial B2B services such as banking, insurance and consulting.

Low levels of digital skills limit adoption of digital solutions

The promotion of digital skills is essential to enable citizens and entrepreneurs to participate in, and contribute to, an increasingly digitalised world. It is a prerequisite for making labour markets more inclusive, as ICT literacy is generally associated with higher labour market participation and wages. The transition to a truly digital business culture is not possible without an adequately skilled workforce, which possesses digital foundation skills, such as the ability to use digital technologies. To design policies that bridge the digital divide and prepare for the digital transformation, policy makers must understand which types of skills help people get the most out of digital technologies, enable their diffusion and increase their impact on productivity. In this regard, four main categories emerge:

- **Foundation skills**, such as literacy and numeracy, enabling the development and acquisition of higher order cognitive skills needed for the digital economy. These foundation skills will help individuals navigate through an environment of fast and ever-changing technologies, as well as increasingly long working lives.
- **Generic digital skills** for all workers, related to the use of digital technologies for professional purposes such as accessing information online or using software.
- **Advanced technical skills** for digital specialists (e.g. skills needed for the production of IT products and services such as programming, developing applications, managing networks).
- **Complementary skills** to work in a digitalised environment, including cognitive skills, interpersonal skills (information processing, self-direction, problem solving, communication), as well as managerial and organisational skills.

Digital skills in general population

A lack of digital skills continues to pose a significant barrier to digital transformation in Azerbaijan. While more than 65% of the population possesses basic ICT skills allowing them to perform digital operations such as sending an e-mail or copying files, Azerbaijan significantly lags behind its regional peers and OECD countries with regards to the share of population with standard and advanced digital skills. Only 0.7% of the population possess advanced ICT skills, which include knowledge of programming languages and the ability to write a computer programme. This is considerably lower than the EU-8 and OECD averages of 4.4% and 6.8%, respectively (ITU, 2021[40]) (see Figure 19).

Acquiring digital skills by self-teaching remains the most prevalent method to acquire ICT skills in Azerbaijan, indicating the limited ability of education system to equip its population with relevant digital skills. In terms of knowledge acquisition, 32.4% of respondents – nearly a third – reported that they acquired their digital skills through learning-by-doing, 26.8% reported educational institutions, 12.1% had acquired them through training courses, and 5.5% reported having gained digital literacy skills through vocational training (The State Statistical Committee of the Republic of Azerbaijan, 2019[21]).

Figure 19. ICT skills in EaP countries

% of individuals by skill level (2019 or latest year available)

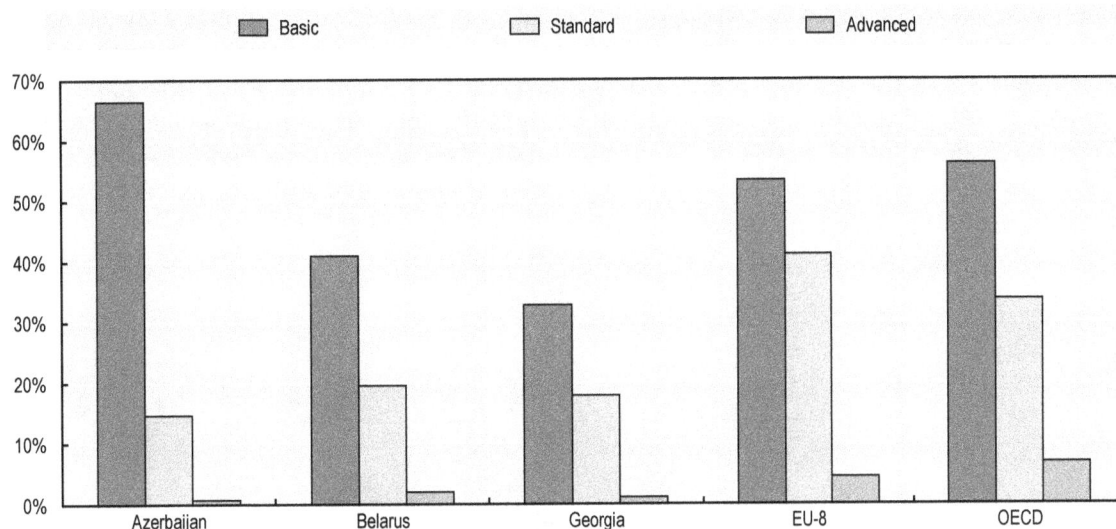

Note: Basic ICT skills are defined as the ability to copy or move files and folders, use copy and paste tools to duplicate and move information within a document, send e-mails with attached files and transfer files from computers and devices.
Source: (ITU, 2021[40]).

The lack of digital skills limits citizens' use of the internet. In a survey conducted by the State Statistical Committee in 2019, 21.8% of respondents reported "lack of skills" as the primary reason for not having an internet access at home: the second biggest obstacle after the costs related to IT equipment (32.2%) (see Figure 20).

Figure 20. Reasons for unavailability of home internet access

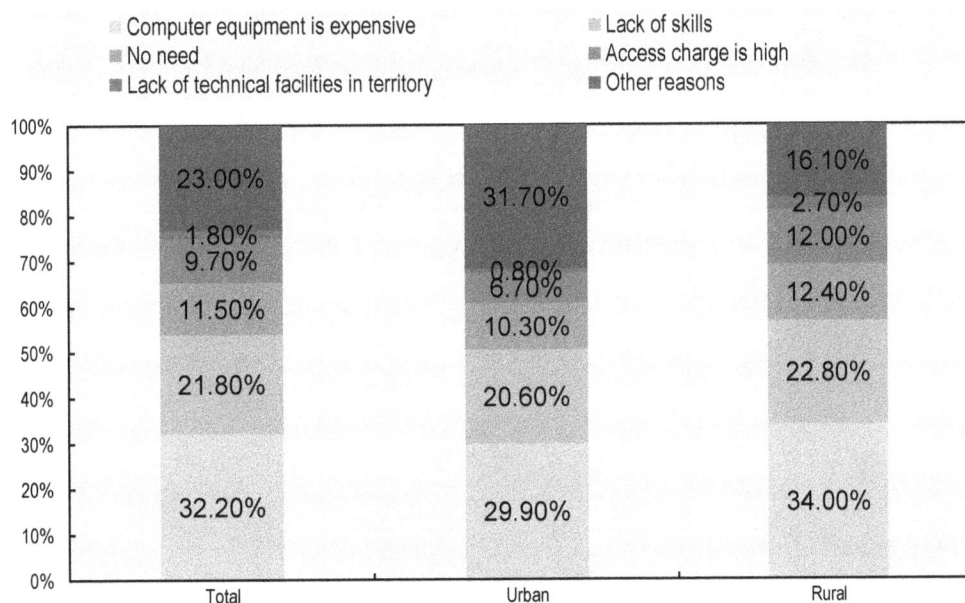

Source: (State Statistical Committee of Azerbaijan, 2020[5]).

The education system can play a crucial role in fostering digital skills

The foundations for digital skills are laid in schools, starting with primary education. However, with rapidly evolving technologies, overly specialised skills tend to become obsolete over time and curricula are rarely flexible enough to allow for ongoing changes (OECD, 2020[41]). Therefore the emphasis should be given to development of foundational skills (literacy and numeracy) and should be complemented by targeted digital literacy educational programmes. According to OECD's Programme for International Student Assessment (PISA), which measures 15-year-olds' ability to use their reading, mathematics and science knowledge and skills to meet real-life challenges, Azerbaijan's students performed below the EaP and OECD averages in all the areas (see Figure 21). It is important to note that only students from Baku participated in the 2018 PISA assessment.

Figure 21. OECD PISA 2018 results

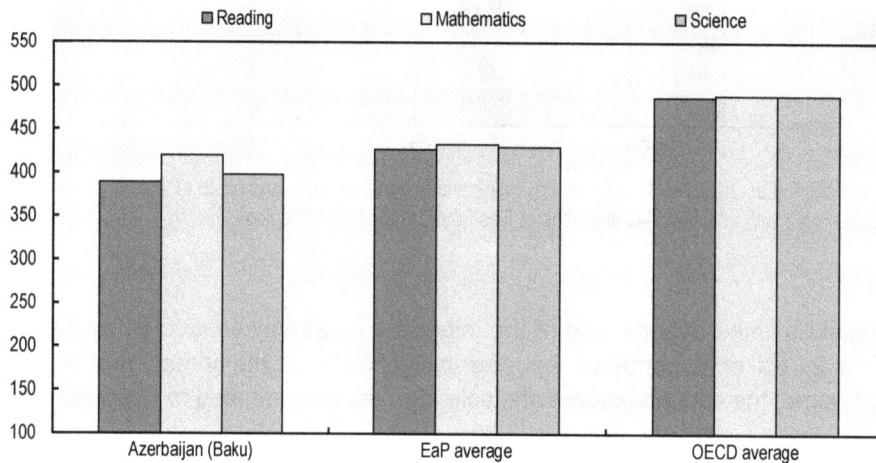

Note: Data for Armenia is not available.
Source: OECD, PISA 2018 Database.

While there is a number of initiatives supporting development of digital skills (see the following section), Azerbaijan did not put in place a dedicated educational framework for fostering digital skills from initial schooling onwards. Azerbaijan lags behind the OECD average in the number of computers available per student: whereas the computer-student ratio in schools was 0.8 for OECD countries in 2018 – meaning there was almost one computer available at school for every 15-year-old student – the ratio was just over 0.5 in Baku.[6] This is lower than in Ukraine, but greater than in other EaP countries (see Figure 22).

---

[6] Nation-wide data unavailable.

Figure 22. Number of computers per student at school (2018)

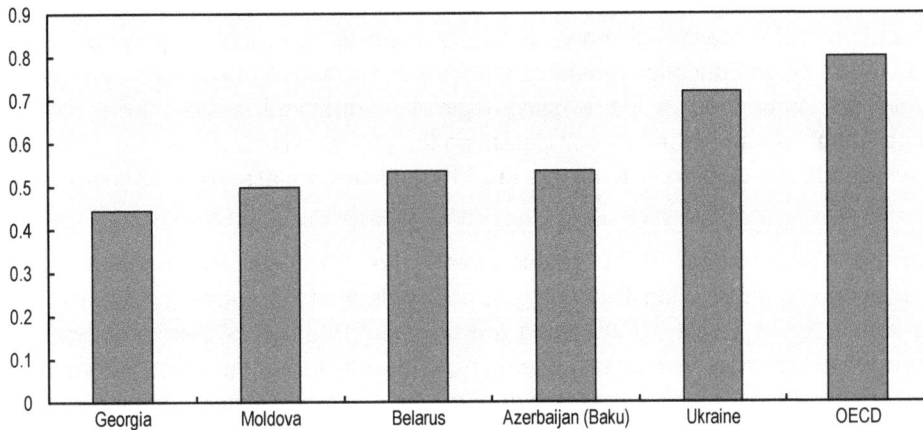

Source: (OECD, 2018[42]).

Looking at the higher education system, the statistics for recent graduates with university degrees indicate a high degree of acquisition of digital skills. In 2019, over half (53.9%) of new graduates with a Bachelor's degree in Azerbaijan received a degree in a Science, Technology, Engineering and Math (STEM) field. Some 21.5% of new graduates received a degree in "technical and technological", 20.8% in "economics and management", 3.7% in "natural sciences" and 7.9% in "health, welfare and services" (The State Statistical Committee of the Republic of Azerbaijan, 2019[21]). Nevertheless, current 15-year old high-school students in Azerbaijan, show low interest in work as ICT professionals in the future compared to their peers in OECD and other EaP countries (see Figure 23).

Figure 23. ICT graduate rates and expectations to work as ICT professionals

% (2019, or latest year available)

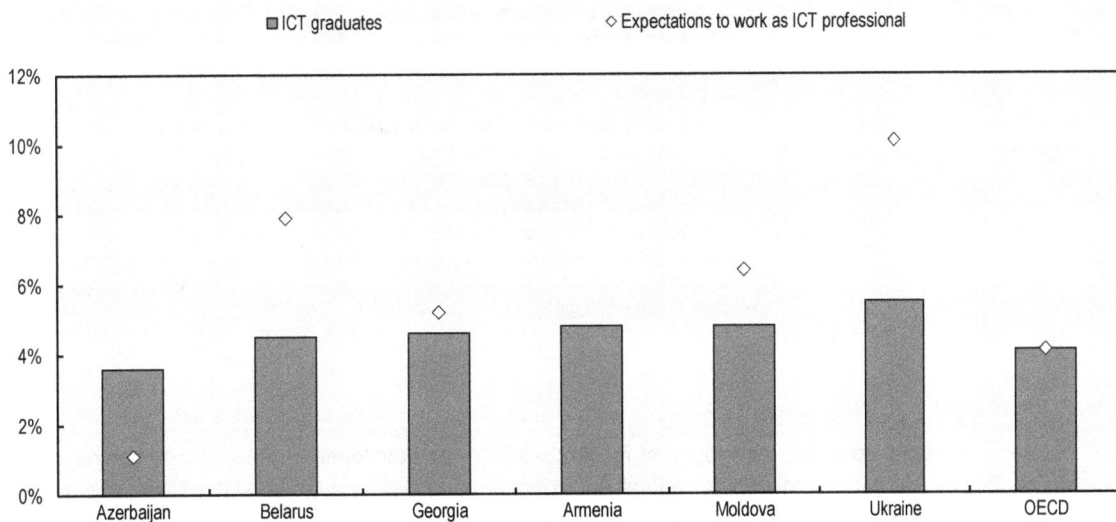

Note: Students expecting to work as ICT professionals at 30 y.o. (% of 15 year olds).
Source: (UNESCO Institute for Statistics, 2019[43]) -Percentage of graduates from tertiary education graduating from ICT programmes (2019; 2017 for Belarus); (OECD, 2018[42]).

Building digital skills is among policy priorities

Digital skills and competences are to a certain extent reflected in policies and strategies that relate to all levels of education in Azerbaijan (primary, secondary and tertiary) including vocational education and training (VET). The Law on Education regulates the roles of the state and education institutions in delivering it. Digital skills are embedded in the existing legislation (national qualifications framework), general education legislation, as one of the key competences for VET and lifelong learning. The NQF for Lifelong Learning, approved by the Cabinet of Ministers in 2018, outlines digital skills in all levels of education (ETF, 2020[44]).

In terms of promoting digital skills development, the Strategic Roadmap for Development of Telecommunication and Information Technologies acknowledges the necessity of enhancing digital skills. It envisages converting to e-schools, meaning a more extensive use of electronic books and seminars, open-access educational materials, distance learning and website-based exams; creating ICT courses for teachers to keep up with the rapidly increasing demand for digital skills, and updating the evaluation of ICT skills of graduates and teachers. The Ministry of Education has also created a digital teaching material platform that contains electronic versions of books and other curriculum materials, as well as a curriculum management information system. It has also introduced a digital skills pilot programme at secondary schools, aiming to introduce coding and programming languages as part of compulsory curriculum for students. Table 4 provides examples of initiatives promoting digital skills development in Azerbaijan.[7]

Table 4. Main initiatives to promote digital skills development amongst the general population

Initiative	Responsible Institution	Description
Digital Skills Project	Ministry of Education	Skills project for students in secondary schools involved 6 500 students in 45 schools in Baku in the 2017-2018 academic year. In 2019, 26 000 5th and 6th grade students from 71 schools were involved in the project in Baku and Ganja. Also under this project, 23 500 students from 65 different schools in Baku and 2 500 students from 6 schools in Ganja are studying computer science in an updated format, which gives students a solid foundation of algorithmic thinking and logic, design skills and programming.
Information-Communication Technologies Application and Training Centre	Ministry of Digital Development and Transport	Provides training and ICT application services to the population, as well as to public and private enterprises. In 2017, the Centre established the "E-Government" project for young people, and in 2019 the number of students studying at the Centre exceeded 1 000. The Centre provides four types of training programmes: certified trainings (Microsoft, Cisco, Oracle, CompTIA); professional trainings (MS Office, Project Management, ICT Network/System; Programming); corporate trainings (digital skills and other programmes); and ICT lab organised corporate training programmes.
Innovation and Digitalisation Agency Azerbaijan	Ministry of Digital Development and Transport	Offers STEM courses to children and students. Courses provide participants with fundamental skills in robotics, science, technology, engineering, chemistry, mathematics, programming and digital art. The Agency has been operating since 2012, having been established by the decree of the President of Azerbaijan with the purpose of ensuring sustainable development and competitiveness of the economy, and the expansion of Azerbaijan's ICT sector. The Agency was established through the reorganization and in the form of a merger of the National Nuclear Research Center CJSC, public legal entity Innovation Agency and High Technologies Research Center under the Ministry.

---

[7] The "Strategy on social-economic development for 2022-2026" was developed in the context of "Azerbaijan 2030: National Priorities on the social-economic development". Encouraging the increase of competitive human capital and of space for modern innovations was identified as a priority, and one of the main related goals is fostering a "creative and innovative society". Moreover, on the basis of the Decree of the President of the Republic of Azerbaijan on "Improvement of the management in the sphere of digital transformation" dated 27 April 2021 No 1325 the Ministry of Digital Development and Transport.elaborated the project "the Conception of digital transformation in the Republic of Azerbaijan".

Initiative	Responsible Institution	Description
Public-private initiatives	n.a.	BP, Alqoritmika and leading banks operating in Azerbaijan play an important role in digital skills development through supporting ICT training programs and establishment of their own IT academies.

Source: (Ministry of Education of Azerbaijan, 2019[45]); (Innovation and Digitalisation Agency Azerbaijan, 2021[46]).

Promoting the adoption of digital solutions by SMEs

Public institutions and private actors providing enterprise support have an important role to play in supporting the digital transformation of SMEs in all industries, helping them overcome the size-related barriers that hamper their access to information, finance, training and quality advisory to progress in their digital transformation agenda. In particular, the following types of support can boost adoption of digital solutions:

- **Awareness raising and information support** – Small enterprise owners are often not aware of benefits (and risks) associated with digitalisation. Awareness raising campaigns and organisation of events promoting digitalisation can nudge entrepreneurs to explore and implement digital solutions. In addition, entrepreneurs are often unaware of existing support programmes that can help them to discover their digitalisation potential, build digital skills or invest into digital solutions.
- **Skills and capacity building** – Policymakers have several tools at their disposal to help build digital skills in SMEs, ranging from the digital diagnostic tools to help SMEs identify their digitalisation deficiencies, training and workshops, and more tailored approaches such as consulting and advice services.
- **Financial support** – Lack of internal funds and restricted access to external finance are often among the main obstacles preventing SMEs from investing into digitalisation. In this context, governments can provide SMEs with grants, loans with preferential interest rate or vouchers that could incentivise entrepreneurs to reach out for external advice or consulting.

Multiple initiatives aim to boost SME digitalisation in Azerbaijan, but comprehensive support programmes are yet to be implemented

Since the adoption of 12 Strategic Roadmaps for the National Economy in 2015, Azerbaijan has made significant improvements in enhancing the SME business support infrastructure and launched a number of financial and non-financial support programmes to boost SME development. The majority of these programmes are implemented by agencies under the supervision of the Ministry of Economy, Ministry of Digital Development and Transport, and the State Agency for Public Service and Social Protection.

Existing support programmes focus mostly on informational support for SMEs, provision of training and consultancy services, and financial support through grants and loans with preferential interest rates. While there is no targeted programme supporting adoption of digital solutions by SMEs from non-ICT sectors, digitalisation is embedded into the existing business support programmes. However, limited co-operation among various providers of digitalisation support services and the absence of a comprehensive digitalisation support programme covering various aspects of financial and non-financial support slow down the uptake of digital solutions by SMEs.

Non-financial support for SME digitalisation remains limited

SMBDA is the main institution providing non-financial support for SMEs

SMBDA operates as a public legal entity under the supervision of the Ministry of Economy. In 2020, the Agency employed 164 staff and operated with a budget of AZN 20 mil (Euro (EUR) 10 mil) financed from the state budget (OECD, 2021[47]). The SMBDA is providing SME support services via its operators that include SME houses, SME Development Centres and SME friends (see Figure 24 for the organisational structure of the SMBDA). While SME digitalisation is among the strategic priorities of the Agency, it does not provide financial and non-financial support programme targeted specifically to digitalisation.

Figure 24. Organisational structure of Small and Medium Business Development Agency

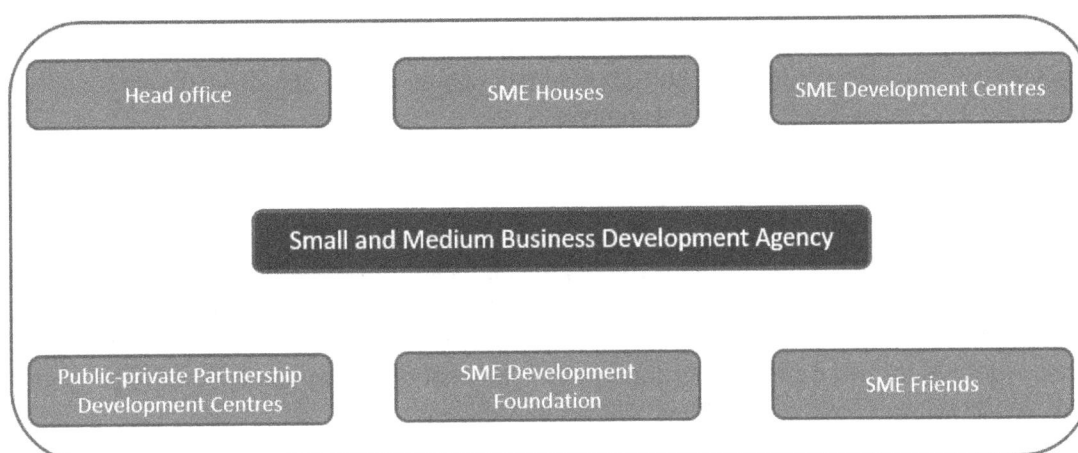

Source: Authors based on https://smb.gov.az/.

SME development centres have the potential to boost SME digitalisation

SME Development Centres provide complex non-financial support services for entrepreneurs with the aim of improving management practices, boosting SME skills and providing targeted advisory and consulting services. SME Development Centres provide training and consultancy services in the areas of management, marketing, legal issues, etc. (see Table 5).

Table 5. Areas of training and consulting services provided by the SME Development Centres

Training services	Consulting services
Starting a business	Support in accessing sales channels
Soft skills	Marketing tips
Project and financial management	Business planning and modelling
Corporate law	Accounting services
Sales	Legal advice and services
Marketing	
Digital skills	

Source: SME Development Centres (2021), https://kobim.az/az/xidmetler.

The SME Development Centres do not provide targeted training programmes or consulting services focused specifically on building digital awareness and enhancing the ability of SMEs to adopt digital solutions. However, the Centres cover issues related to digital skills and digitalisation more broadly as part of the available training and consultancy services based on ad-hoc needs (e.g. online sales, digital marketing).

As of December 2021 there are 21 SME Development Centres operating in the regions (16 of them launched in 2021), and they represent the main channel through which SMBDA provides its services to SMEs. During the first 9 months of 2021, SME Development Centers provided 1 077 training services to 15 000 SMEs, consulting services to 1 212 SMEs, and supported the development of 178 business plans. All services are provided free of charge and SMEs are not required to co-finance them (OECD, 2021[47]).

While SMBDA significantly boosted the provision of training and consulting services for SMEs, interviews with SME policy makers and experts conducted by the OECD indicated that awareness of SMEs' training needs continues to be limited. This could be partly related to the lack of a systematic approach to the identification of SME needs and growth barriers, including those related to SME digitalisation. Even though SMBDA conducts an annual survey of SMEs to identify overall needs and development priorities, this cannot replace a company-specific needs diagnostic.

While SME Development Centres are under the supervision of the SMBDA, the Agency has only limited control over the scope and quality of services provided since these Centres are run by sub-contractors selected by the SMBDA. The sub-contractors are responsible for the delivery of all services provided in Centres and they determine the scope and type of provided support. This allows for greater flexibility and ability to tailor the services to the specific needs of SMEs in a given region. However, it might also lead to an inconsistent approach to trainings and consultancy services provided across regions and may lower their quality (despite follow-up satisfactory surveys that are performed by each SME Development Centre and which indicated high satisfactory rate among beneficiaries).

SMBDA has also developed a video training platform to increase the training and education opportunities. The platform offers a total of 180 training videos, presentation of training topics, relevant self-assessment tests and information support on issues including starting a business, soft skills, corporate law, project management, finance, sales, marketing, tourism and organization of the export process.

SME houses provide G2B and B2B services including those supporting digitalisation

Small and medium business houses (SME houses) are structural units of the SMBDA operating as a one-stop-shop providing G2B and B2B services. They offer services of several state institutions such as the State Custom Committee, Ministry of Economy (including State Tax Office), Ministry of Digital Development and Transport. With regards to services related to SME digitalisation, the SME houses provide information on the services of the SMBDA and its training programmes, the Entrepreneurship Development Fund, information on the activities of the Innovation and Digital Development Agency, but also issuance of e-signature. Currently there are two operational SME houses, in Khachmaz and Yevlakh (SMBDA, 2021[48]). While the SME houses provide important information and services support for SMEs, their potential to boost SME digitalisation is limited by their focus on general services but also due to their regional limitations (currently only 2 offices).

In addition to the two SME houses, the SMBDA launched an e-SME house portal, which aims to provide some services provided by SME houses online. Entrepreneurs that want to use the services of the e-SME house have to request a personal electronic account and are able to authorise all interactions using their e-signature. Entrepreneurs can use the portal to pay customs duties, payments for government services, but also use various financial "B2B", banking, insurance and consulting services (SMBDA, 2021[48]).

The Innovation and Digital Development Agency aims to boost digitalisation, but with the primary focus on the ITC sector

The establishment of the Innovation and Digital Development Agency in 2018 under the supervision of the Ministry of Digital Development and Transport represents an important milestone in shaping the business support environment in Azerbaijan. The Agency was created by merging the ICT Fund and the High-Tech Park Azerbaijan. Its main objective is to assist individuals and legal entities in obtaining modern technologies and technological solutions, promote innovation-oriented research and innovative projects (including start-ups), provide them with financial support and promote innovation (Innovation and Digitalisation Agency Azerbaijan, 2021[46]).

The Innovation and Digital Development Agency oversees two high-tech parks located in Mingachevir and Pirallahi island, Barama Innovation and Entrepreneurship Centre and Symbiosis Technical Business Incubator, and is expected to establish an Innovation House which should provide complex services for innovative companies. However, while the above-mentioned initiatives promote ICT development and development of the high-tech sector and therefore contribute to digital transformation and diversification of the economy, SMEs operating in non-ICT sectors will not benefit from their services as they are not in the primary target group.

ABAD supports digitalisation of micro enterprises in Azerbaijan's regions

ABAD – Easy Support for Family Business is a public legal entity established in 2016 under the State Agency for Citizen Services and Social Innovations. Its main objective is to support the development of family businesses to increase employment, support business formalisation and facilitate socio-economic development in the regions. ABAD centres in Baku, Quba, Balakan, Masalli, Imisli and Sheki support family businesses mainly in the sectors of handicrafts and food processing and packaging. Currently, services are being provided to over 350 clients, of whom approximately 50% are women.

Services provided by ABAD include business planning, marketing, training, branding and design, financial accounting, legal assistance and, most importantly, sales and equipment. With regards to digitalisation, ABAD provides businesses with an e-commerce platform (https://abad.gov.az/?locale). While there is no special programme targeting SME digitalisation, adoption of digital solutions is embedded in existing support, focusing, for example, on online marketing and e-commerce.

Financial support for SME digitalisation holds its promise

Restricted access to external finance continues to be one of the major barriers preventing SME development. According to an OECD enterprise survey carried out in 2018, 58% of surveyed SMEs considered insufficient access to finance the main barrier to their growth (OECD, 2019[38]). The often intangible nature of digital projects exacerbates the access to finance issues already faced by many SMEs. Banks' credit departments are often unable or unwilling to assess the potential values and risks of a digital project and low financial literacy among SMEs further exacerbates the problem. As the alternative sources of financing and FinTech are still in their infancy, SMEs are often unable to access external financing.

Although government-sponsored financial support for SMEs in Azerbaijan has improved in recent years, existing support mechanism have limited scope and are not used to support purchase and adoption of digital technologies by SMEs.

The Entrepreneurship Development Fund operating under the Ministry of Economy provides, through commercial banks, loans to SMEs with preferential interest rate (5% p.a.). The size of loans is between AZN 50 000 (EUR 25 000) and AZN 1 million (EUR 500 000). In the first 9 months of 2021, the Entrepreneurship Development Fund provided financing for 1152 companies, most of them operating in the agricultural sector. The Fund started to implement a new strategy, which was adopted in January 2021 and identifies the financing priorities until 2023, which include telecommunication projects and digitalisation.

While SMBDA is primarily focusing on non-financial support, the Agency also has a grant mechanism in place to award SMEs with grants of up to AZN 20 000 (EUR 10 000). The grant programme is not yet fully operational and in in the first half of 2021 only 15 companies have received the support. However, the SMBDA plans to revamp the programme and will allocate an additional AZN 200 000 (EUR 100 000) until end of 2021 for SME grants.

The Innovation and Digital Development Agency provides financial support for innovative projects, including for commercialising research, as well as for acceleration programmes such as Idea to Business and Fast Track. In the past, the ICT Fund distributed grants, with a maximum amount of AZN 50 000 (EUR 25 000). The Innovation and Digital Development Agency plans to increase the maximum amount to AZN 500 000 (EUR 250 000), to support ambitious innovation projects that have large scope and scale. The Innovation and Digital Development Agency's role as a facilitator of innovation activities is not entirely clear or well defined, as some of its mandates overlap with those of other government authorities with responsibilities for science and innovation (UNECE, 2020[49]).

Sector-specific digitalisation strategies and support programmes are still underdeveloped

While the adoption of digital technologies has a great potential to improve performance of SMEs across all sectors, the implications of digitalisation are likely to differ across different sectors, which calls for industry-specific strategies and support programmes. For example, intelligent and digitally connected machinery can enable the development of precision farming, which can boost productivity in the agricultural sector. On the other hand, logistics and online marketing and sale can boost performance of SMEs operating in the retails sector.

Azerbaijan's institutions do not conduct sector-specific studies to determine digital maturity of different industries. As a result, sector-specific digitalisation support in Azerbaijan is limited to a few initiatives.

Limited co-ordination among digital ecosystem institutions hinders effectiveness of support

In the last 5 years, Azerbaijan has put in place a number of new institutions and programmes to support private-sector development and spur innovation. However, new policy instruments are not yet fully operational. Both old and newly established authorities lack full capacities to formulate, design and implement initiatives. While this is partly a natural process of building internal capacities, limited co-ordination between innovation agents – enterprise support and innovation agencies, high-tech parks, business incubators, etc. – limits the overall efficiency and effectiveness of existing programmes.

Active involvement of the private sector in the design and delivery of the digitalisation support programmes is very limited. This co-operation can be critical to ensure the quality of provided services, buy-in from the potential support beneficiaries, and better sustainability of the provided services. In addition, as all the programmes are provided free of charge, it limits the uptake of private sector providers of business development services and prevents further development of consultancy market.

Way forward

Policymakers have a key role to play in promoting an efficient and inclusive digital transformation by ensuring that the necessary complementary factors are in place that enable SMEs to both benefit from emerging opportunities and cope with the challenges raised through digital transformation. This involves a range of policy priorities, from improving digital infrastructure and regulatory framework conditions over developing skills and training opportunities to providing targeted advisory and financial support services. This section provides a set of policy considerations that Azerbaijan could use to: (i) promote a whole-of-government approach to digitalisation, (ii) ensure that framework conditions are conducive to SME digitalisation, and (iii) foster the uptake of digital solutions by SMEs.

Objective 1: Promote a whole-of-government approach to digitalisation

Recommendation 1: Leverage "Azerbaijan 2030 Vision" and corresponding mid-term strategies to boost SME digitalisation

The Azerbaijan 2030 Vision adopted in early 2021 provides a unique opportunity for the government to embed digitalisation among strategic policy priorities that can boost diversification, increase competitiveness, reduce inequalities and contribute to overall socio-economic development. Relevant mid-term policy strategies that will set the course for the policy actions until 2025 that are being developed by the line ministries should include a set of policy objectives and actions that will contribute to the creation of an ecosystem conducive to digital transformation of the private sector and its SMEs in particular.

Azerbaijan could galvanise its commitment to digital transformation by adopting a National Digital Strategy that would set priorities and objectives for digitalisation across policy areas and support it with appropriate budgetary allocations. The strategy should acknowledge that digitalisation is not only relevant for the ICT sector and should address policy priorities across a number of relevant policy areas (e.g. connectivity, education, entrepreneurship, public services).

It will be important that sectoral mid-term policy strategies prepared under the Azerbaijan 2030 Vision target the main challenges related to SME digitalisation in Azerbaijan such as connectivity, regulatory framework and cybersecurity, digital culture and skills, and uptake of digital solutions by SMEs. Policy recommendations outlined in this note could provide a general direction for policy-makers when setting-up objectives and designing policy strategies. Box 2 outlines five steps that could be followed to develop a digital transformation strategy.

Establish a governance approach that supports effective co-ordination

- Set up an effective steering and co-ordination mechanism for digital transformation taking into account the country's specificities, culture and institutions.

- Assign clear responsibilities for strategic co-ordination and operational co-ordination for the development and implementation of a national digital transformation strategy (DTS).

Articulate a strategic vision and ensure coherence

- Articulate a strategic vision that provides direction on identifying the main priorities and scoping of the main objectives of a DTS.

- Ensure coherence between a DTS and other related domestic and international digital strategies and policy objectives.

Assess key digital trends, related policies and regulations

- Monitor key digital trends, including by international benchmarking, to identify opportunities and challenges to be addressed by a DTS.

- Evaluate the effectiveness of current strategies and/or policies, identify gaps and/or incoherence, and scope objectives for a DTS.

Develop a comprehensive and coherent strategy

- Leverage the governance approach, the strategic vision, and insights from monitoring and evaluation to develop a comprehensive and coherent DTS.

- Engage all relevant actors in developing a DTS, including different parts and levels of government, non-governmental stakeholders and international partners.

Implement the strategy successfully

- Anticipate and address implementation challenges related to institutions and policy frameworks, social preferences and (lack of) administrative capacity.

- Issue an action plan with specific measures, clear responsibilities, budget, timeframes and measureable targets to successfully implement the DTS.

Source: (OECD, 2020[23]).

To ensure that the mid-term strategies are effective in steering policy, it is important that they are accompanied by corresponding action plans that set out realistic and measurable objectives. It is crucial that the progress along each action can be assessed using process and result key performance indicators (KPIs). KPIs should be: (a) specific – it should be clear what the indicator measures; (b) measurable – the indicator should ideally be expressed in numerical terms (e.g. values, ratios, growth rates); (c) achievable – the indicator should be realistic; (d) relevant – the indicator should be closely linked to the objectives of individual measures; and (e) trustworthy – the indicator should be based on reliable and replicable data (OECD, 2019[38]).

Recommendation 2: Improve co-ordination among institutions responsible for digital transformation

While the Ministry of Digital Development and Transport has been the main institution responsible for policies related to ICT, such as the implementation of the ICT Strategic Roadmap, as overall policy plans are moving towards digital uptake by firms, digital training, and cross-border e-commerce, the need to involve other institutions is becoming apparent. However, a lack of co-ordination among relevant institutions is preventing existing policy initiatives from achieving their full potential. In this context, Azerbaijan could improve co-ordination at all levels of decision-making and policy implementation to promote policy coherence, boost the impact and effectives of existing policies, increase utilisation of digitalisation support programmes and infrastructure, and benefit from spill-over effects.

Azerbaijan could consider establishing a Digitalisation Commission – a co-ordination platform that would bring together all relevant stakeholders involved in the design and implementation of digitalisation related policies and support programmes. Such a platform should have a high-level mandate and could be established, for example, under the Prime Minister's Office. It could have its own and independent technical secretariat providing the members with analysis and background documents (see Figure 25). The Digitalisation Commission should bring together all relevant public institutions, private sector representatives and academia. Its main objective should be to serve as a forum for dialogue and co-ordination on digitalisation-related policies, but could also have a mandate to recommend formulation of policies, provide comments on draft laws and regulations and provide recommendations for its members and non-members on policy initiatives related to the digitalisation agenda.

Figure 25. Example of the governance structure of the Digitalisation Commission

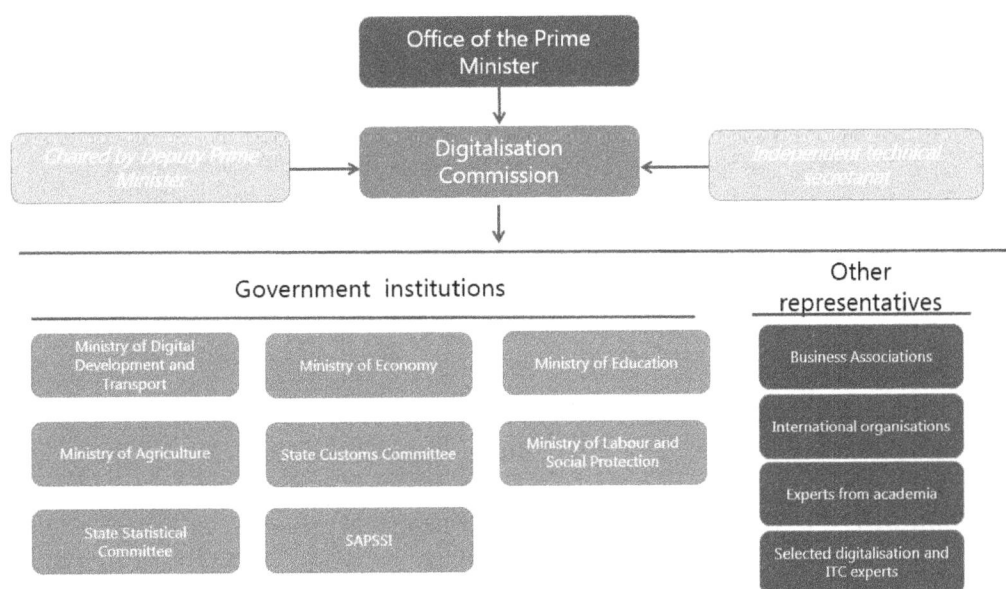

Source: Authors own work based on the project Working Group meetings.

Recommendation 3: Improve data collection on SME digitalisation to support evidence-based policy making

The limited availability of data measuring SME digitalisation is one of the main constraints to evidence-based policy making. Availability of statistical data is also important in the context of the preparation of the mid-term strategies in the context of Azerbaijan 2030 Vision as critical data are needed to define the right KPIs and therefore measure the impact and effectiveness of policy actions.

The State Statistical Committee of Azerbaijan currently collects only a small number of indicators related to digitalisation of the private sector, mostly relating to companies' internet access. The State Statistical Committee in co-operation with relevant public and private sector authorities could consider expanding the range of collected SME digitalisation-related data. The data collection should focus on diffusion of digital technologies among SMEs, cybersecurity and cybercrime, but also on e-commerce and online payments penetration. Where possible and relevant, data could be disaggregated by the enterprise size class and sector. Adapted from the OECD Survey on ICT Usage by Businesses, Table 6 provides example of core indicators that could be collected by the State Statistical Committee (OECD, 2015[50]).

Table 6. Core indicators on SME digitalisation

Area	Indicator
Connectivity	Persons employed regularly using a computer at work (as a % of persons employed)
	Enterprises with (fixed/mobile) broadband (as a % of total enterprises)
	Connection speed (distribution)
	Persons employed with access to the Internet (% of persons employed)
	Persons employed provided with Internet enabled portable devices (% of persons employed)
Website	Enterprises having a website (% of enterprises)
	Enterprises with a website allowing for online ordering (% of enterprises – total & w/website)
Information management tools	Enterprises using ERP, CRM (plus EDI and RFID) software (% of total – by technology/application)
	Enterprises sharing electronically supply management information with suppliers/customers (% of total, by type of partner)
E-commerce	Enterprises conducting e-sales (as a % of enterprises)
	E-sales value by platform (EDI, web) and customer (B2X) (% of total turnover of enterprises, including by platform and customer)
	Enterprises conducting e-purchases (as a % of enterprises)
	E-purchases value by platform (EDI, web) (% of total purchases of enterprises, including by platform)
Security and privacy	Security breaches/incidents encountered (% of enterprises by occurrence)
	Formal policy to manage ICT privacy risks (% of enterprises)

Source: (OECD, 2015[50]).

Objective 2: Ensure that framework conditions are conducive to SME digitalisation

Recommendation 1: Continue improving digital infrastructure

Access to high-speed and reliable internet is essential for digital transformation. Azerbaijan should focus on meeting its policy objectives of improving overall connectivity, addressing the regional gaps in access to technology and the internet. Azerbaijan could consider implementing policies in line with the *OECD Recommendation on Broadband Connectivity*[8] and provide high-speed broadband at reliable prices by:

- Promoting internet access for all and fostering the adoption of advanced broadband services at affordable prices;

---

[8] https://legalinstruments.oecd.org/en/instruments/OECD-LEGAL-0322

- Reducing barriers to broadband access through regulation and policies to enable investment, while safeguarding competition and investment incentives; and

- Promoting measures to strengthen the resilience of communication networks, such as network diversity and redundancy, to reduce connection disruptions (OECD, 2021[51]).

To improve regional connectivity, Azerbaijan could implement policies that encourage investment in resilient infrastructure, which in turn would provide affordable network coverage and access to broadband internet. Azerbaijan can boost connectivity in rural and remote areas by investing in high-speed fixed networks or increasing private investment through measures such as competitive tendering, tax exemptions, low interest loans, public support or lower spectrum fees.

Azerbaijan could work to further promote competition in all markets for network infrastructures and services with non-discriminatory policies to expand and achieve user choice for access to internet at affordable prices. In this context, the government could implement measures to reduce administrative barriers to trade and investment.

Recommendation 2: Strengthen the regulatory framework for digitalisation

It is critical that Azerbaijan ensures that the recently established National Regulatory Agency for telecommunications sector under the Ministry of Digital Development and Transport is independent and has sufficient financial and human resources to fulfil its mission. The NRA should promote efficient competition, investment and consumer interests with development of electronic communications markets, services and networks. Recommendations provided by *Gap assessment of Azerbaijan regulatory system in the field of electronic communications* prepared under the EU4Digital project could be taken into account as good practices to follow when drafting the charter for the NRA (EU4Digital, 2020[52]).

Azerbaijan could also adopt a National Cybersecurity Strategy. The Strategy should set a clear objectives and actions to improve the security and resilience of national information infrastructures and services, and should include SME-specific targets and objectives. The European Union Agency for Cybersecurity[9] provides an implementation guide, good practice examples and an evaluation framework for national cybersecurity strategies, on which Azerbaijan could draw (see Box 3).

To support adoption of security measures by SMEs, the authorities could also establish a national certification scheme for digital security. The scheme could provide a series of "best practices" that enterprises can implement in their own operations or in the design of their products and services. Upon completing the requisite steps, enterprises could receive a certification that can signal to consumers or business partners the level of digital security of the enterprise or its services.

As the low cybersecurity awareness among SMEs is (globally) one of the main barriers to wider use of protection measures, the Cyber Academy operating under the Ministry of Digital Development and Transport could strengthen efforts to increase awareness of digital security targeting, specifically SMEs. Those efforts should aim to provide guidance and examples of affordable solutions that, if adopted, would reduce SME digital security exposure and potential losses.

---

[9] https://www.enisa.europa.eu/topics/national-cyber-security-strategies/national-cyber-security-strategies-guidelines-tools

Box 3. Developing a cybersecurity strategy

In 2016, the European Union Agency for Cybersecurity outlined specific steps for developing a national cyber security strategy to increase the global resilience and security of national ICT assets.

1. Set the vision, scope, objectives and priorities: setting clear objectives and priorities is crucial for developing a cybersecurity strategy. During this step, the government should define the vision and scope of the objectives, and develop a roadmap for their implementation.

2. Follow a risk assessment approach: carrying out a national risk assessment and aligning the objectives of the strategy with national security needs allows to focus on the most important challenges with regards to cyber security.

3. Take stock of existing policies, regulations and capabilities: it is necessary to take into account international cybersecurity requirements. This will help align the cybersecurity strategy with international standards and identify important gaps.

4. Set a clear governance structure: a governance framework should define the roles, responsibilities and accountability of all relevant stakeholders. A public body or an interagency working group should be defined as the co-ordinator of the strategy.

5. Identify and engage stakeholders: public stakeholders ensure the safety and security of the nation's critical infrastructures and services. Selected private entities should be part of the development process as they are likely the owners of critical information infrastructures and services.

6. Establish trusted information-sharing mechanisms: government should properly define the information-sharing mechanism and the underlying principles and rules that govern the mechanism. Owners of critical infrastructures could share with public authorities their input on mitigating emerging risks, threats and vulnerabilities.

Source: (European Union Agency for Cybersecurity, 2016[53]).

Azerbaijan could work to improve the overall framework for e-commerce by increasing financial inclusion and the use of online banking, and by strengthening the logistics for e-commerce by further decreasing time needed for cross-border trade It could improve the logistics of parcel delivery by establishing consolidated central distribution networks with centralised warehouses. This would reduce delivery times for both domestic and cross-border delivery of commercial items, and allow for more efficient use of e-commerce (EU4Digital, 2021[35]).

Azerbaijan could also take measures to improve customer protection. For instance, based on the directives applied in the EU, Azerbaijan could require e-commerce platforms to inform their customers of their rights and label paid product placements when customers search for items. Implementing such measures could strengthen customer protection and improve trust in e-commerce platforms in the country.

Recommendation 3: Support the development of digital skills

Even though Azerbaijan is implementing a number of initiatives supporting digital skills development for students and the general population, a comprehensive policy framework to build digital skills from early childhood that would engage a wide range of relevant stakeholders is lacking. Azerbaijan could consider comprehensive and co-ordinated approaches driven by cross-governmental digital education strategies, with scattered initiatives implemented by different institutions and agencies. While such initiative could be led by the Ministry of Education, it essential that other institutions such as the Ministry of Digital Development and Transport and the Ministry of Economy are also part of the process.

To better understand education and training needs, Azerbaijan could conduct a skills needs assessment, accompanied by a skills anticipation exercise. Such efforts could help determine the existing supply of a digitally skilled labour force, assess skills demand from companies, identify skills gaps and develop policies to address digital skills requirements. In this context, International Telecommunication Union's (ITU's) *Digital Skills Assessment Guidebook* provides practical information on how to assess supply and demand for digital skills (ITU, 2020[54]).

Besides further developing programmes offering digital skills development for the general population, responsible institutions should increase awareness among SMEs and the population of the availability of such training and education opportunities. SMEs are often unaware of existing training options or consider them too costly. SMBDA could take the lead in informing SMEs of credible training options and help them find the best and most appropriate trainings or skills development initiatives.

Objective 3: Promote uptake of digitalisation among SMEs

Azerbaijan could put in place a digitalisation eco-system that would support adoption of digital solutions by SMEs by: (i) guiding them through an assessment of their digital maturity; (ii) developing sector-specific digital plans outlining a "digitalisation roadmap" from digital basic level to digital maturity; (iii) providing financial support to tackle the lack of resources; and (iv) facilitating access to quality training and advisory services (see Figure 26) (OECD, 2021[13]).

Figure 26. A policymaker's blueprint to accelerate digital transformation

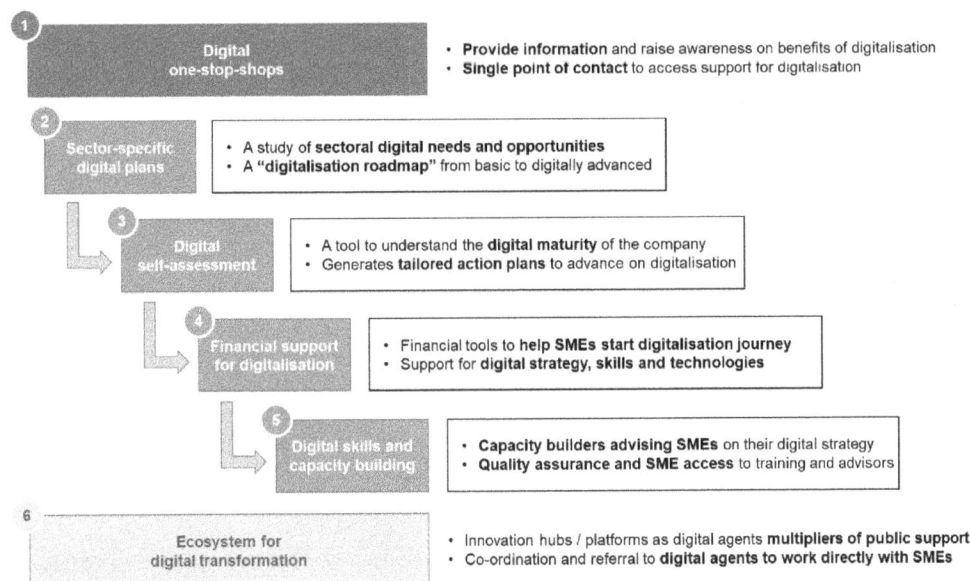

Source: (OECD, 2021[13]).

Recommendation 1: Promote digital culture and increase digital awareness among entrepreneurs

A lack of awareness among entrepreneurs about the benefits of digitalisation is one of the main barriers to more widespread use of digital solutions among SMEs. Therefore relevant public institutions, such as the

SMBDA and the Innovation and Digital Development Agency, could implement programmes to promote digital awareness among SMEs operating in non-ICT sectors. The main objective of such initiatives is to communicate to entrepreneurs and managers the benefits (and risks) associated with adoption of digital solutions for their businesses and how digital transformation can help increase productivity.

The SMBDA could implement awareness-raising campaigns and organise awareness-raising events and competitions to boost the digital awareness of SMEs. The SME Friends and SME Development Centres should act as "SME digitalisation ambassadors" and use their networks and communication channels to increase interest in digital solutions among non-ICT SMEs.

Recommendation 2: Understand SME digitalisation needs

Developing a good understanding of SMEs' digitalisation needs is a prerequisite for the delivery of tailored solutions that will have a positive impact on SME operations. A macro-analysis of the state of digitalisation for different sectors could be performed to establish a baseline and identify sectoral priorities for delivering state support programmes in a context of limited resources. To understand the level of digital maturity of an industry, surveys could be conducted to collect information on a series of indicators capturing both the depth of digital culture and the adoption of digital solutions in different business areas.

The SMBDA could deepen the scope of the survey it conducts among SMEs to find out about barriers to their operations and training needs and link findings of the survey to the delivery of support services provided by its business support network. Focus group meetings and formal consultations with the business community could also accompany the survey and support demand- and need-driven provision of support services. The surveys and focus group meetings should also enquire about the adoption of digital solutions by SMEs and barriers preventing SMEs from broader use of digital technologies.

The SMBDA could also design an online digital maturity self-assessment tool. The tool would enable companies to assess their digital maturity and identify their development needs and challenges. The platform could also recommend relevant actions that companies could take to improve marketing, selling, production, and administrative processes, and to undergo digital transformation. The tool could help the SMBDA (and SME Development Centres in particular) better understand needs of individual companies and devise appropriate training and mentoring programmes to target these needs. The digital maturity self-assessment tool should serve as the starting point for SMEs to begin a digital transformation tailored specifically to their needs. The adoption of a digital maturity self-assessment tool should also be designed according to the relevance of each sector, and should serve as a reference for SMEs to determine the level of digital maturity that their peer sectorial companies have. Box 4 describes a self-assessment questionnaire on SME digitalisation implemented by the Moldovan Organisation for Economic Co-operation and Development (ODIMM), the Moldovan SME Development Agency.

In June 2020, ODIMM (Moldovan agency for development of small and medium-sized enterprises) launched the SME Digitalisation Programme to support the digital transformation of SMEs. Under this programme, SMEs can benefit from the following types of support: 1) digital maturity test; 2) based on the results of the test, targeted capacity building and trainings in 5 different modules, tackling 19 topics such as strategic planning, online marketing and customer support; 3) access to business vouchers for further advice and consulting up to Moldovan Leu (MDL) 20 000 (EUR 960), and 4) grants up to MDL 200 000 (EUR 9 600 to cover expenses related to digitalisation (most often costs related to hardware purchases).

SMEs begin by taking a self-assessment questionnaire in order to determine their level of digital maturity. The test evaluates an SME's level of online presence, e-commerce, transport and logistics, client services and process digitalisation. Each of the topics contain specific questions and sub-questions to find out more details on an SME's use of platforms, what type of customers they have and what information they rely on. Based on the results of the questionnaire, SMEs are classified as either low/beginner in their digitalisation process, medium/intermediate or advanced. The results of the assessment allows SMEs as well as ODIMM to determine which areas of business require more intervention and would benefit from business vouchers and training.

By spring 2021, 466 companies had received training and 180 had been financially supported through grants and business vouchers.

Source: (ODIMM, 2021[55]).

Recommendation 3: Reinforce the provision of non-financial support services

While digitalisation-related training and advice is embed into existing training modules, Azerbaijan could consider expanding non-financial support for SME digitalisation. SMBDA (through its network of SME Development Centres) could implement programmes focusing on boosting SME ability to implement digital solutions. The Agency could consider providing dedicated programmes focusing only on SME digitalisation that could cover the following aspects of digitalisation (OECD, 2021[13]):

- **Strategy and digital culture.** The digital transformation should be addressed at the core of the SME's business objectives and strategic planning, as well as its culture and organisational values.
- **Customer Relationship.** Business should exploit digital tools to improve customer experience, knowledge and engagement.
- **Organisation and talent.** Enterprises should embrace new ways of work offered by digitalisation. The main benefits of the digitalisation of the enterprise's organisation and developing digital talents are increased employee engagement, agility, lower employee turnover rate, improved company culture and better preparedness.
- **Technology.** Digital technologies are a centrepiece of a successful digital transformation. Digital devices and instruments can simplify employees' work and reinforce the potentials of business operations. The main benefits of adopting digital technologies are reduced costs, greater flexibility and innovation, improved service levels, improved resilience to external threats.
- **Products and services.** Digitalisation brings novel techniques of doing business or refining business models, adding value to the customer based on new knowledge acquired through digitally collected data.

To maximise the impact of digitalisation support services and benefit from spill-over effects, SMBDA could consider implementing a complex financial and non-financial support programme combining digital self-assessment (see previous recommendation), digital skills and capacity development and financial support instruments (see the following recommendation). Box 5 describes "SME Go Digital", a programme implemented by Singapore's Infocomm Media Development Authority (IMDA), which combines various forms of support.

Box 5. "SME Go Digital" programme in Singapore

In 2017, IMDA established the SMEs Go Digital programme to help Singapore's SMEs build their digital culture and fully reap the potential of digital technologies. It also aims to raise awareness amongst SMEs about the potential that digital technologies bring, and the growth opportunities in digital economy.

The programme works through providing support through sector-specific Industry Digital Plans (IDPs), which guide SMEs with a step-by-step guide on digital solutions to adapt, and provide relevant training for their employees, tailored for their specific skill levels at different stages of their growth. The IMDA supports SMEs in adopting recommended digital solutions and increases awareness about the benefits of digitalisation. SMEs that are part of the programme also have the option to apply for the Productivity Solutions Grant (PSG) through the Business Grants Portal set up by the IMDA in order to receive funding of up to 80% of the costs associated with adopting digital solutions.

In 2019, IMDA in partnership with Enterprise Singapore (ESG) launched the Start Digital Initiative to help newly incorporated SMEs adopt digital solutions. The agency also works to increase awareness about the benefits of digitalisation, working with SMEs to identify their specific digitalisation needs and tailor recommendations such that it fits the digitalisation priorities of the client company.

Since the programme's launch in 2017, more than 75 000 companies have adopted digital solutions from the programme.

Source: (SMEs Go Digital, 2021[56]).

Recommendation 4: Boost financial support for SME digitalisation

Azerbaijan could boost the adoption of digital solutions by SME by improving their ability to access external financing. The Entrepreneurship Development Fund and SMBDA could consider expanding their existing financial support programmes or launch new initiatives targeting SME digitalisation specifically. For example, the Entrepreneurship Development Fund could provide loans with preferential interest rates for SMEs that aim to purchase digital software and hardware and SMBDA could provide small grants for companies that want to establish an online presence. Box 6 outlines the grant scheme provided by Enterprise Estonia to boost adoption of digital solution by Estonian SMEs.

> ## Box 6. Financial support for SME digitalisation in Estonia
>
> ### Enterprise Estonia
>
> Enterprise Estonia established a grant programme, aimed specifically for manufacturing and mining firms to boost adoption of digital technologies. This is an application-based grant, which supports digitalisation activities such as staff training, purchase and implementation of materials necessary for automation, implementation of cyber security and protection systems, and many others. Only firms with annual sales of over EUR 200 000 are eligible for the grant.
>
> The grant programme provides digitalisation diagnostic grants amounting to EUR 15 000, digital roadmap grants of 15 000 EUR and digitalisation grants of 20 000 EUR to successful applicants. The programme works directly with SMEs to identify gaps in their digitalisation that need to be addressed, and employs experts to list technical solutions to eliminate gaps in the supply chain. The goal is to make the process more efficient, and support the technical needs of the companies. Selected SMEs receive support from the programme for the next 3 years.
>
> There is no strict criteria in order to qualify for the grant, however, SMEs need to demonstrate that they have been active in the last 2-3 years prior to application, meaning they have active operations and interact with customers. In 2018 and 2019, the programme received approximately 130 applications for the grant. This number decreased in 2020, largely due to the pandemic-related measures interrupting operations. By September 2021, the programme had received almost 150 applications.
>
> Source: (Enterprise Estonia, 2021[57]).

Azerbaijan should also continue improving SME access to non-government sources of external finance. In the context of SME digitalisation, it should address challenges related to using intangible assets as collateral and address banks' negative bias towards digitalisation projects. The government should also create a regulatory framework for alternative providers of external financing and continue improving financial literacy of SMEs.

Recommendation 5: Ensure the quality of the support services provided

Azerbaijan should ensure that the support programmes provided by public institutions fulfil requirements on their quality, impact and effectiveness. Systematic monitoring and well-planned evaluations of support programmes, especially those providing continuous training and consulting services, can provide decision makers with necessary evidence and feedback on the quality and impact of provided support services. It should be based on measurable indicators and on the level of satisfaction. It will provide information on the impact of the services and can also serve as a change-management tool in the context of future support.

During the implementation of support programmes, service providers should keep records on process indicators such as: (i) number of self-assessment reviews completed, (ii) number of SMEs provided with support, (iii) number of participants attending each training session, (iv) level of satisfaction of participants with trainings and consulting sessions.

Monitoring and evaluation should start before the implementation of each programme and would continue after its delivery against a set of KPIs. KPIs should measure the outcomes for the beneficiaries and assess the effectiveness of the programme in supporting adoption of digital solutions by programme beneficiaries. Table 7 provides examples of KPIs evaluating digitalisation support programmes.

Table 7. Example of KPIs for digital support programmes

Target	KPIs
Adoption of digital solutions	Adopted digital solutions following the participation in the digitalisation support programme (e.g. ERP, CRM)
E-commerce	Annual online sales (in AZN)
	Share of online sales on total sales
Online marketing	Online marketing platforms utilised
	Share of digital marketing expenditures on total marketing expenditures (%)
Cybersecurity	Measures implemented to increase cybersecurity

Note: selection of KPIs depends on a type and scope of the evaluated support programme and its objectives
Source: Author work based on the project Working Group meeting.

For services provided by public institutions, but outsourced to consultants and external providers, responsible institutions should ensure that selected external providers meet qualification criteria to deliver the tasks in required quality. For example, the SMBDA is entirely outsourcing management and delivery of support services provided by SME Development Centres. Moreover, providers of the Centres have relative autonomy in identifying type and scale of provided services. While this gives them flexibility to react to local specificities and SME needs, it calls for the SMBDA to ensure that services provided by SME Development Centres are aligned with national SME and digitalisation policy priorities. The SMBDA could also provide SME development Centres with methodological guidelines what should be covered by training programmes and, if relevant, provide them with training materials and know-how. To ensure that services in the SME Development Centres are provided according to high-quality standards, the SMBDA could impose minimum quality requirements for consultants delivering services in the Centres.[10] Box 7 outlines the quality assurance system for consultants implemented by Austrian SME Development Agency.

Box 7. Consultants assurance system and certification in Austria

In 2017, the Federal Ministry of Digitalisation and Business Location (BMDW) in co-operation with the Austrian Chamber of Commerce established the Austrian Institute for SME Research (KMU) Digital initiative: a programme designed to support SMEs' digitalisation. The programme provides financial support for consulting services and investments in digitalisation projects for SMEs. KMU Digital is funded by the federal government. The Austrian Chamber of Commerce (WKO) is responsible for implementation of advisory funding.

KMU Digital promotes individual consulting for Austrian SMEs. Analyses and strategy consultations may only be carried out by certified consultants, and consultants are required to comply with content-related quality criteria and formal regulations. Further, KMU Digital digitalisation consultants are required to have a certification tailored to the respective topic:

- Digital Consultant (focus on business models and processes (including resource optimisation))
- E-Commerce & Social Media Consultant
- E-Commerce & Social Media Expert
- Data & IT Security Expert (CDISE)

---

[10] Currently, the SMBDA surveyes the entrepreneurs to identify their needs. On the basis of the information collected, the Agency determines the scope of work and the terms of reference for the activities, and a tender is held. The winning operator companies are selected to organize the activities of SME Development Centers.

- Digital Public Administration Expert

KMU Digital provides webinars and trend cards for its consultants with information on the programme and current trends. The agency does not provide funding for training or certification for consultants, however it does provide them with information about grants available for further professional development in digital skills. Consultants are required to document their completed consultations online in a structured report, which should contain further recommendations for the client.

The EU Commission positively highlighted KMU Digital in its "Country Report Austria 2019", noting its positive impact on SMEs in Austria.

Source: (KMU.Digital, 2021[58]).

Recommendation 6: Leverage existing business and innovation support infrastructure to create an eco-system conducive to digitalisation

Since 2016, Azerbaijan has significantly expanded its business and innovation support infrastructure by establishing and consolidating relevant agencies (e.g. SMBDA, Innovation and Digital Development Agency), and building a network of business incubators, high-tech and industrial parks, and other business innovation agents. In addition, the Ministry of Economy has promoted the establishment of business associations bringing together companies operating in the similar sectors. Policy-makers should try to maximise the impact of this eco-system by improving co-ordination among innovation agents and promote spill-over effects.

The SMBDA could monitor all existing initiatives and not only help SMEs to navigate in the existing support eco-system and direct them towards relevant programmes and events, but also actively participating in their design and encourage co-operation. For example, SME Development Centres, which are responsible for digitalisation training and consultancy services, could closely co-operate with Electronic Security Centre operating under the Ministry of Digital Technologies and Transport when delivering training or advice on cybersecurity.

The SMBDA agency should engage in close co-operation with all the relevant business associations operating in Azerbaijan to better understand sector-specific needs of SMEs, design demand-driven support programmes, increase confidence among SMEs regarding the benefits of the support programmes and benefit from these communication channels with SMEs.

Public support programmes should also be provided as a way to unlock demand for privately-provided consulting services which go beyond the scope of the SMBDA in terms of depth and sophistication. In this context, the SMBDA should be cautious with free-of-charge provision of support services. While providing free services can boost the demand and interest among SMEs in training and mentoring services, it can also distort the private sector consultancy market and obstruct its development.

References

Asian Development Bank (2019), *Azerbaijan: Country Digital Development Overview*, https://www.adb.org/sites/default/files/institutional-document/484586/aze-digital-development-overview.pdf. [26]

Azintelecom (2020), *Azintelecom*, https://azintelecom.az/en/2020/02/21/2nd-international-cyber-security-week-to-be-held-in-azerbaijan/. [28]

Central Bank of Azerbaijan (2021), *Central Bank of the Republic of Azerbaijan Electronic Services Portal*, https://www.e-cbar.az/News/Info/5809331?culture=en. [36]

Centre for Analysis on Economic Reforms and Communication (2018), *"STATE PROGRAM ON EXPANSION OF DIGITAL PAYMENTS IN THE REPUBLIC OF AZERBAIJAN FOR 2018-2020"*, https://monitoring.az/assets/upload/files/eea155986deceec851611c23f.pdf. [31]

Economist Intelligence Unit (2021), *Azerbaijan: country report*. [7]

E-Gov (2021), *e-gov.az*, https://www.e-gov.az/en/content/read/5. [29]

EIB (2020), *A bigger digital divide*, https://www.eib.org/en/stories/growing-digital-divide. [20]

Enterprise Estonia (2021), *Services*, https://www.eas.ee/teenused/?lang=en&eas=182. [57]

ETF (2020), *Digital Factsheet: Azerbaijan*, https://www.etf.europa.eu/sites/default/files/2021-03/digital_factsheet_azerbaijan.pdf. [44]

EU4Digital (2021), *Recommendations Proposed for eCommerce Environment Harmonisation in EaP Countries: Republic of Azerbaijan*, https://eufordigital.eu/wp-content/uploads/2021/04/eCommerce-report-%E2%80%93-Recommendations-proposed-for-eCommerce-environment-harmonisation-in-the-EaP-countries-Republic-of-Azerbaijan.pdf. [35]

EU4Digital (2020), *Gap Assessment of Azerbaijan regulatory system in the field of electronic communications*, https://eufordigital.eu/wp-content/uploads/2021/04/Gap-assessment-of-Azerbaijan-regulatory-system-in-the-field-of-electronic-communications.pdf. [52]

European Union Agency for Cybersecurity (2016), *NCSS Good Practice Guide*, https://www.enisa.europa.eu/publications/ncss-good-practice-guide. [53]

IMDA (2021), *Industry Digital Plans*, https://www.imda.gov.sg/programme-listing/smes-go-digital/industry-digital-plans. [18]

IMF (2021), *WORLD ECONOMIC OUTLOOK DATABASES*, https://www.imf.org/en/Publications/SPROLLS/world-economic-outlook-databases#sort=%40imfdate%20descending. [33]

Innovation and Digitalisation Agency Azerbaijan (2021), *Innovation Agency*, https://innovationagency.az/en/innovation-agency/. [46]

International Fund for Agricultural Development (2019), *Azerbaijan*, https://www.ifad.org/en/web/operations/w/country/azerbaijan. [6]

ITU (2021), *Digital Trends in the Commonwealth of Independend States Region 2021*, https://www.itu.int/en/publications/ITU-D/pages/publications.aspx?parent=D-IND-DIG_TRENDS_CIS.01-2021&media=electronic. [40]

ITU (2021), *Global Cybersecurity Index 2020*, https://www.itu.int/epublications/publication/global-cybersecurity-index-2020/en/. [25]

ITU (2020), *Digital Regulation Platrform*, https://digitalregulation.org/regulatory-governance-and-independence/. [27]

ITU (2020), *Digital Skills Assessment Guidebook*, https://academy.itu.int/main-activities/research-publications/digital-skills-insights/digital-skills-assessment-guidebook. [54]

ITU (2019), *5G - Fifth Generation of Mobile Technolgies*, https://www.itu.int/en/mediacentre/backgrounders/Pages/5G-fifth-generation-of-mobile-technologies.aspx. [17]

KMU.Digital (2021), *KMU Digital - The Austrian Digitalisation Initiative for SMEs*, https://www.kmudigital.at/Content.Node/kampagnen/kmudigital/the-austrian-digitalization-initiative-for-smes.html. [58]

Ministry of Education of Azerbaijan (2019), *Ministry of Education Republic of Azerbaijan*, https://edu.gov.az/en/news-and-updates/16036. [45]

National Certification Services Centre (2018), *Statistics*, http://e-imza.az/en/statistics. [30]

ODIMM (2021), *"Digital Upgrate" Has Started - The Educational Program for Digitizing SMEs*, https://odimm.md/en/press/press-releases/4936-digital-upgrade-has-started-the-educational-program-for-digitizing-smes. [55]

OECD (2021), *Advancing digital business transformation in Eastern Partner countries*, https://www.oecd.org/eurasia/Covid19_%20Advancing%20digital%20business%20transformation%20in%20the%20EaP%20countries.pdf. [13]

OECD (2021), *OECD SME Agency survey in EaP countries*. [47]

OECD (2021), *Recommendation on Broadband Connectivity*, https://legalinstruments.oecd.org/en/instruments/OECD-LEGAL-0322. [51]

OECD (2021), *The Digital Transformation of SMEs*, OECD publishing, https://doi.org/10.1787/bdb9256a-en. [19]

OECD (2020), *COVID-19 crisis responses in Eastern Partner countries*, https://www.oecd.org/coronavirus/policy-responses/covid-19-crisis-response-in-eu-eastern-partner-countries-7759afa3/. [2]

OECD (2020), *Digital economy outlook*, OECD Publishing, https://www.oecd-ilibrary.org/science-and-technology/oecd-digital-economy-outlook-2020_bb167041-en. [23]

OECD (2020), *SME Policy Index: Eastern Partner Countries*, https://www.oecd-ilibrary.org/docserver/8b45614b-en.pdf?expires=1627997816&id=id&accname=ocid84004878&checksum=7367F601B58A49CFB68DFE549B109E62. [37]

OECD (2020), *What Students Learn Matters: Towards a 21st Century Curriculum*. [41]

OECD (2019), *An Introduction to Online Platforms and Their Role in the Digital Transformation*, OECD Publishing, Paris, https://dx.doi.org/10.1787/53e5f593-en. [14]

OECD (2019), *Azerbaijan: Driving Diversification through Strengthened Entrepreneurship*, https://www.oecd.org/eurasia/competitiveness-programme/eastern-partners/Azerbaijan-Driving-Diversification-through-Strengthened-Entrepreneurship.pdf. [38]

OECD (2019), *Digital for SMEs Global Initiative*, https://www.oecd.org/going-digital/sme/aboutus/D4SME-Brochure.pdf. [12]

OECD (2019), *Measuring Digital Transformation: A Roadmap for the Future*, https://www.oecd.org/going-digital/mdt-roadmap-measuring-internet-of-things.pdf. [16]

OECD (2019), *OECD Blockchain Primer*, https://www.oecd.org/finance/OECD-Blockchain-Primer.pdf. [15]

OECD (2019), *SBA assessment 2020*, https://www.oecd-ilibrary.org/sites/42efd1f2-en/index.html?itemId=/content/component/42efd1f2-en. [9]

OECD (2018), *Bridging the rural digital divide*, https://read.oecd-ilibrary.org/science-and-technology/bridging-the-rural-digital-divide_852bd3b9-en#page2. [24]

OECD (2018), *PISA*, OECD. [42]

OECD (2015), *The OECD Model Survey on ICT Usage by Businesses*, https://www.oecd.org/sti/ieconomy/ICT-Model-Survey-Usage-Businesses.pdf. [50]

OECD et al. (2020), *SME Policy Index: Eastern Partner Countries 2020: Assessing the Implementation of the Small Business Act for Europe*, OECD Publishing, https://doi.org/10.1787/8b45614b-en. [10]

Peillon, S. and N. Dubruc (2019), *Barriers to digital servitization in French manufacturing SMEs*, https://reader.elsevier.com/reader/sd/pii/S2212827119306195?token=7A0AA9C36B7495B1B2738700C9461CE2E55295F4A58A6D4602DA13FEC9F943951B37E6025FD05601877C712680620E67&originRegion=eu-west-1&originCreation=20210924133535. [11]

Report News Agency (2015), *Number of Cyber Attacks in Azerbaijan Increases Annually by 30%*, https://report.az/en/ict/the-number-of-cyber-attacks-in-azerbaijan-increases-annually-by-30/. [59]

SMBDA (2021), *Small and Medium Business Development Agency of the Republic of Azerbaijan*, https://smb.gov.az/en. [48]

SMEs Go Digital (2021), *Infocomm Media Development Authority*, https://www.imda.gov.sg/programme-listing/smes-go-digital. [56]

State Statistical Committee of Azerbaijan (2020), . [5]

Statista (2021), *Statista*, https://www.statista.com/outlook/digital-markets. [32]

The State Statistical Committee of the Republic of Azerbaijan (2019), *Share of micro, small and medium entrepreneurship subjects in the value of goods loaded, works executed, services performed, rendered by economic activity types*, https://www.stat.gov.az/source/entrepreneurship/?lang=en. [21]

UN (2021), *United Nations e-Government Knowledgebase*, https://publicadministration.un.org/egovkb/en-us/Data/Country-Information/id/64-Georgia-Country/dataYear/2010. [39]

UNECE (2020), *Innovation Policy Outlook 2020: Eastern Europe and South Caucasus*, https://unece.org/sites/default/files/2021-06/UNECE_Sub-regional_IPO_2020_Publication.pdf. [49]

UNESCO Institute for Statistics (2019), *National Monitoring*, UNESCO Institute for Statistics. [43]

USAID (2021), *Challenges and opportunities for SME development in Azerbaijan, Belarus, Georgi and Ukraine*, https://www.smedevelopment-project.de/Bilderpool/SME_Development_Project_2021/SME_Development_Report.pdf. [22]

World Bank (2021), *Competition and Firm Recovery Post-COVID-19*, https://openknowledge.worldbank.org/bitstream/handle/10986/36296/9781464818028.pdf. [4]

World Bank (2021), *Enterprise Survey*, http://www.enterprisesurveys.org. [3]

World Bank (2019), *World Integrated Trade Solution (WITS)*, https://wits.worldbank.org/CountryProfile/en/Country/AZE/Year/LTST/TradeFlow/EXPIMP/Partner/WLD/Product/All-Groups. [8]

World Bank (2017), *Financial Inclusion Index*, World Bank. [34]

Worldometer (2021), *Worldometer*, https://www.worldometers.info/coronavirus/country/azerbaijan/. [1]

Annex A. Project implementation

The objective of this project is to support the capacity of policy makers in Azerbaijan to promote the adoption of digital solutions amongst SMEs. The project is implemented by the OECD in co-operation with the Ministry of Economy and Small and Medium Business Development Agency of Azerbaijan.

Data collection for the project was supported by the following institutions that were members of the Project Advisory Group: the Ministry of Economy of Azerbaijan; Agency for Agro Credit and Development, Ministry of Agriculture of Azerbaijan; Ministry of Digital Development and Transport of Azerbaijan; Central Bank of Azerbaijan; Azerbaijan Service and Assessment Network (ASAN); Azerbaijan State Statistical Committee; and the National Confederation of Entrepreneurs Organisations of Azerbaijan.

Data collection was also supported by regular exchanges with representatives from the Small and Medium Business Development Agency (SMBDA) and the Ministry of Economy of Azerbaijan and other memebrs of the Project Advisory Group, as well as extensive desk research.

Working group meetings

The OECD organised two Working Group meetings in June and October 2021. The meetings brought together a wide range of stakeholders involved in the design and implementation of SME policies, including policy makers and business associations from Azerbaijan, the OECD members countries, OECD and international experts, and the EU.

First Working Group (June 2021)

The objective of the meeting was to discuss policies to support the digital transformation of SMEs in Azerbaijan with members of a working group established within the framework of the project "Promoting SME digitalisation in Azerbaijan".

The meeting was opened with remarks from Mr Mehman Abbas, the Deputy Chairman of the Small and Medium Business Development Agency of Azerbaijan, and Ms Ulviya Abdullayeva, the Project Manager of the Delegation of the European Union to Azerbaijan. Mr Patrik Pruzinsky from the OECD Eurasia Division then introduced the project *Promoting SME Digitalisation in Azerbaijan,* and discussed its main features, implementation processes and objectives.

During the first session, public and private sector representatives from Azerbaijan presented current trends and challenges of SME digitalisation in Azerbaijan, as well as planned policy initiatives and support programmes aiming to boost digitalisation of the SME sector. The panel brought together remarks from Mr Mehman Abbas, Deputy Chairman of the Small and Medium Business Development Agency of Azerbaijan; Mr Tamerlan Taghiyev, Director of the Centre for Analysis and Coordination of the 4IR, Ministry of Azerbaijan; Ms Leyla Mammadova, Deputy Chairperson, Agency for Agro Credit and Development (AKIA), Ministry of Agriculture of Azerbaijan; Mr Eldar Jahangirov, Team Leader on conceptualisation of national digitalisation, Ministry of Transportation, Communications and High Technologies of Azerbaijan; Mr Farid Osmanov, Executive Director, Central Bank of Azerbaijan; Mr Mehdi Javadov, Deputy Director, e-Gov Development Centre, State Agency for Public Service and Social Innovations; Mr Nuru Suleymanov, Director, Department of National Accounts and Macroeconomic Statistics, Azerbaijan State Statistical

Committee; and Mr Vugar Zeylanov, Vice President, National Confederation of Entrepreneurs (Employers) Organizations of Azerbaijan (ASK).

The second panel focused on ways and approaches to support digital transformation of SMEs based on international good practices. Mr Raido Lember, Business Development Manager, Enterprise Estonia, outlined the main features of Estonia's approach to SME digitalisation support. Mr Jesus Lozano, IT entrepreneur and senior expert on SME digitalisation, shared benefits of digital transformation and the role of government in supporting digital transformation.

Second Working Group (October 2021)

The objective of the second Working Group meeting was to discuss preliminary findings and policy recommendations of the porject with members of the Working Group within the framework of the project "Promoting SME Digitalisation in Azerbaijan".

The meeting was opened with remarks from Mr Elmar Isayev, Head of Secretariat of the Small and Medium Business Development Agency of Azerbaijan and Ms Ramila Aslanova from the EU Delegation to Azerbaijan. Mr Patrik Pruzinsky and Ms Maria Zelenova of the OECD Eurasia Division then presented the preliminary findings and draft policy recommendations of the project. The presentation covered the strategic approach to SME digitalisation, the framework conditions for SME digitalisation and digital skills, and policies to support the uptake of digital solutions by SMEs.

Mr Jesus Lozano, IT entrepreneur and senior expert on SME digitalisation, presented a blueprint for a programme to support uptake of digital technologies by SMEs, accompanied by practical examples based on international best practices and personal experience.

Following that, participants exchanged their views on the presented findings and draft policy recommendations, and discussed latest government initiatives to support SME digitalisation. Representatives from the Ministry of Economy, SMBDA, Ministry of Digital Development and Transport, State Agency for Public Service and Social Innovations (ASAN), Central Bank of Azerbaijan, and State Statistical Committee participated in the discussion.